May Your Song Always Be Sung
(An Introduction to Bob Dylan's Poetry)

Joel-Isaiah McIntyre

To Jesús Rodríguez Rivero
"May God bless and keep you always"
(Forever Young, Bob Dylan)

1. Introduction

It's a very common experience that someone reads first time some Dylan's verses and nothing of it makes sense, for instance, "There must be some way out of here," said the joker to the thief / "There's too much confusion, I can't get no relief / Businessmen, they drink my wine, plowmen dig my earth / None of them along the line know what any of it is worth" (All Along The Watchtower). Even if the reader tries to read those lines in the context of the whole song, he still doesn't get the point: ""There must be some way out of here," said the joker to the thief / "There's too much confusion, I can't get no relief / Businessmen, they drink my wine, plowmen dig my earth / None of them along the line know what any of it is worth" / "No reason to get excited," the thief, he kindly spoke / "There are many here among us who feel that life is but a joke / But you and I, we've been through that, and this is not our fate / So let us not talk falsely now, the hour is getting late" / All along the watchtower, princes kept the view / While all the women came and went, barefoot servants, too / Outside in the distance a wildcat did growl / Two riders were approaching, the wind began to howl" (All Along The Watchtower).

Readers face similar difficulties when it comes to making some sense of songs like Mr. Tambourine Man: "Though I know that evenin's empire has returned into sand / Vanished from my hand / Left me blindly here to stand but still not sleeping / My weariness amazes me, I'm branded on my feet / I have no one to meet / And the ancient empty street's too dead for dreaming / Hey! Mr. Tambourine Man, play a song for me / In the jingle jangle morning I'll come followin' you" (Mr. Tambourine Man). Reading through the whole lyrics of the song doesn't help too much, actually there are paragraphs even more difficult to interpret: "Take me on a trip upon your magic swirlin' ship, / My senses have been stripped, my hands can't feel to grip, / My toes too numb to step, wait only for my boot heels / To be wanderin'. / I'm ready to go anywhere, I'm ready for to fade / Into my own parade, cast your dancing spell my way, / I promise to go under it." (Mr. Tambourine Man).

Some Dylan's songs are locked: "Oh, what'll you do now, my blue-eyed son? / Oh, what'll you do now, my darling young one? / I'm a-goin' back out 'fore the rain starts a-fallin' / I'll walk to the depths of the deepest black forest / Where the people are many and their hands are all empty / Where the pellets of poison are flooding their waters / Where the home in the valley meets the damp dirty prison / Where the executioner's face is always well hidden / Where hunger is ugly, where souls are forgotten / Where black is the color, where none is the number / And I'll tell it and think it and speak it and breathe it / And reflect it from the mountain so all souls can see it / Then I'll stand on the ocean until I start sinkin' / But I'll know my song well before I start singin' / And it's a hard, it's a hard, it's a hard, it's a hard / It's a hard rain's a-gonna fall." (A Hard Rain's A Gonna Fall). Poets always deliver their stuff in a way that is difficult to follow, and so Dylan does too. One of the key points to unlock some poems is to read them in the right context. As long as we read Dylan in the right context we will be able to make more sense of his lyrics.

In the following pages we want to propose a methodology to unlock some Dylan verses by putting them in the right context, how? By trying to track down specific links between specific Dylan's verses throughout his poetry, which is going to give us a context to understand better what Dylan is talking about.

Why are we going to focus on links between some of his verses? Because Dylan said that he was extending the line: "last thing I thought of was who cared about what song I was writing. I was just writing them. I didn't think I was doing anything different. I thought I was just extending the line" (Speech on MusiCares Person of the Year, 2015). What does it mean? It means basically that he was following the pattern of those who were singing and writing before him, which is probably why Dylan wrote: "I gotta make my own statement bout this day/ I gotta write my own feelings down the same way they did it before me in that used t be day" (For Dave Glover, June 1963). From the beginning of his career as a singer-song writer, Dylan was following folk tradition and getting inspiration from folk singers. Robert Shelton was right when he said "every cult figure stands on the shoulders of those who came before" (Shelton, 2011:18). It turns out that if you try to track down the links of Dylan's songs with American traditional music and then with his own lyrics, you will understand what he's singing and writing about. And that's what we are going to do in the following pages. We need a first reading of Dylan's poetry (looking for connexions and links between his verses), that's going to be the first part of this research, and then a second reading, that's going to be the second part of this research, that will be done in the right context that we are going to obtain after our first reading of Dylan's poetry.

All Dylan is in Dylan. If we want to understand him, we have to read him taking into account what he was doing: extending the line. Then, we will be able to hear him and to understand him.

Dylan said once, "people ask why do I write the way I do/ how foolish/ how monsterish/ a question like that hits me…/ it makes me think that I'm doing nothing/ it makes me think that I'm not being heard".

2. "Extending the line": A journey throughout Bob Dylan's studio albums

The process of creating folk songs is about extending the line, as Dylan explains in the latest interview to bobdylan.com: "most everything is a knockoff of something else. You could have some monstrous vision, or a perplexing idea that you can't quite get down, can't handle the theme. But then you'll see a newspaper clipping or a billboard sign, or a paragraph from an old Dickens novel, or you'll hear some line from another song, or something you might overhear somebody say just might be something in your mind that you didn't know you remembered." (Q&A with Bill Flanagan, March 22, 2017, Exclusive to bobdylan.com). It's not the first time Dylan talks about it; he had already said: "All these songs are connected. Don't be fooled. I just opened up a different door in a different kind of way. It's just different, saying the same thing" (Speech on MusiCares Person of the Year, 2015). As Dylan explained during that speech: "Roll the cotton down, aw, yeah, roll the cotton down / Ten dollars a day is a white man's pay / Roll the cotton down/A dollar a day is the black man's pay / Roll the cotton down." If you sang that song as many times as me, you'd be writing "I ain't gonna work on Maggie's farm no more," too. If you'd had listened to the Robert Johnston singing, "Better come in my kitchen, 'cause it's gonna be raining out doors," as many time as I listened to it, sometime later you just might write, "A Hard Rain's a-Gonna Fall." (Speech on MusiCares Person of the Year, 2015); and "Gather 'round, people / A story I will tell / 'Bout Pretty Boy Floyd, the outlaw / Oklahoma knew him well." If you sung all these "come all ye" songs all the time like I did, you'd be writing, "Come gather 'round people where ever you roam, admit that the waters around you have grown / Accept that soon you'll be drenched to the bone / If your time to you is worth saving / And you better start swimming or you'll sink like a stone / The times they are a-changing." (Speech on MusiCares Person of the Year, 2015).

That's how it works, and that's why, when reading Bob Dylan, it's interesting to be attentive to find a source of inspiration that is a new Dylan song's starting point and then expecting further developments. This is what extending the line is all about: a) quote of a preexisting tune or reference to a preexisting tune, either a Dylan's tune or a someone else's tune; b) developing that quote or reference in a new way, adding some elements, coming up with some innovation. For instance, Dylan wrote "Let me eat when I am hungry / Let me drink when I am dry / A dollar when I am hard up / Religion when I die" (Moonshiner, 1961) probably because he knew that preexisting tune "It's a beef steak when I'm hungry / rye whiskey when I'm dry / Green back when I'm hard up / and heaven when I die" (Jack Of Diamonds, 1926); and then, he expressed his own feelings with his own words: "The whole world's a bottle / And life's but a dram / When the bottle gets empty / It sure ain't worth a damn" (Moonshiner, 1961). The starting point is the preexisting tune, then he extends the line on his own way.

That's the way Dylan writes songs. If we are able to see the connexions between his verses, we will be able to read Dylan in the right context. In the following pages we proceed to do a first reading of Dylan's poetry pointing out the links between lines. We will follow the chronological order of his studio albums and some interviews. We have taken the lyrics from bobdylan.com.

—*Bob Dylan (1962)*

Extending the line. It was precisely because Dylan had been repeatedly singing and listening to lines like "I've seen lots of funny men / some will rob you with a six-gun, / and some with a fountain pen" (Pretty Boy Floyd) that he wrote and sang "Now, a very great man once said that some people rob you with a fountain pen" (Talkin' New York). He was familiar with folk material like "I've been hittin' some hard harvestin', I'm tryin' make about a dollar a day" (Hard Travelling), which is why he wrote "well, I got a harmonica job begun to play blowing my lungs out for a dollar a day" (Talkin' New York). He knew lines like "you ask about work and you ask about pay; they'll tell you that they make less than a dollar a day" (1913 Massacre), that led him to write and sing "the man there said he loved m' sound, he was ravin' about how he loved m' sound, dollar a day's worth" (Talkin' New York).

"Talkin' New York" and "Song To Woody" are the only two original songs in Bob Dylan's first album ever released and their lyrics show that he was learning to write about that world of characters fighting to work their lives out under difficult conditions, like "Oh, the gamblin' man is rich an' the workin' man is poor, and I ain't got no home in this world anymore" (I Ain't Got No Home). It was precisely because he knew those lines that he wrote and sang "I'm seeing your world of people and things; hear paupers and peasants and princes and kings" (Song To Woody). He was seeing that world while he listened to and sang folk material like "I've been havin' some hard travelin', way down the road" (Hard Travelling) and that's why he wrote and sang "I'm leaving tomorrow but I could leave today; somewhere down the road someday; the very last thing that I'd want to do is to say I've been hitting some hard travelling too" (Song To Woody). He writes "I'm out here a thousand miles from my home / Walkin' a road other men have gone down" (Song To Woody), which extends the line "A hot and dusty road that a million feet have trod" (Ain't Got No Home, Woody Guthrie).

—*The Freewheelin' Bob Dylan (1963)*

Because he knew that old tune "I'm a rollin' stone all alone and lost / For a life of sin I have paid the cost" (Lost Highway, Hank Williams) he wrote "My mind got mixed with ramblin' / When I was all so young" (Long Time Gone, Bob Dylan, 1962-1964). He knew "And a woman's lies makes a life like mine / On the day we met, I went astray / I started rolling down that lost highway" (Lost Highway, Hank Williams) that led him to write "I once loved a fair young maid / An' I ain't too big to tell / If she broke my heart a single time/ She broke it ten or twelve" (Long Time Gone, Bob Dylan, 1962-1964).

Dylan extends the line and then he follows his own way. For instance, the lyrics of "Lost Highway" includes some advice, "Now boys don't start to ramblin' round / On this road of sin are you sorrow bound / Take my advice or you'll curse the day / You started rollin' down that lost highway"; but Dylan says he cannot give advice to anybody: "If I can't help somebody / With a word or song / If I can't show somebody / They are travelin' wrong / But I know I ain't no prophet / An' I ain't no prophet's son" (Long Time Gone, Bob Dylan, 1962-1964). By the way, in that line Dylan is probably quoting the prophet Amos "I was neither a prophet nor the son of a prophet" (Am 7,14).

That's what you can find constantly throughout Dylan's lyrics, lines on love and the difficulties to succeed at it. In the spirit of "Lost Highway" he wrote many of the songs of "The Freewheelin' Bob Dylan" and other songs he sang and recorded on the early sixties. "I'm walkin' down the highway / with my suitcase in my hand" (Down the Highway). Love is the goal, and it has to be a good one: "Oh you five and ten cent women / With nothin' in your heads / I got a real gal I'm lovin' / And Lord I'll love her till I'm dead / Go away from my door and my window too / Right now" (Bob Dylan's Blues). It is love what makes him to feel motivated, thats why he wrote "And sometimes I'm in the mood, I wanna hit that highway road / but then again, but then again, I said oh, I said oh, I said / oh, babe, I'm in a mood for you" (I'm In A Mood For You). And again the inspiration goes back to tunes like "I've been havin' some hard travelin', way down the road" (Hard Traveling) and other tunes. Love is the reason why Bob Dylan is walking down the road, "Well, I'm a-walkin' down the road / With my head in my hand / I'm lookin' for a woman / Needs a worried man" (Honey, Just Allow Me One More Chance). However, love is difficult to find and actually many of Bob Dylan's tunes on love are about a lost love: "Well, lookin' for a woman / That ain't got no man / Is just lookin' for a needle / That is lost in the sand" (Honey, Just Allow Me One More Chance), and "Lord, I really miss my baby / she's in some far-off land (Down The Highway). Indeed, lost love is what the following lines are talking about: "When your rooster crows at the break of dawn / look out your window and I'll be gone; / you're the reason I'm travelling on" (Don't Think Twice It's all right). Those difficulties in finding love are his trouble: "I been gamblin' so long, Lord / I ain't got much more to lose / right now I'm havin' trouble" (Down the highway). Girl from the North country is also about lost love: "I'm a-wonderin' if she remembers me at all / Many times I've often prayed / in the darkness of my night / in the brightness of my day." In this context, it makes perfect sense that Dylan recorded a traditional tune about lost love, "Baby, please come home / I ain' a-got Corrina, Life don't mean a thing / I just can't keep from crying (Corrina, Corrina). He writes "Well, the ocean took my baby / My baby stole my heart from me" (Down The Highway), which extends the line "I've been out in front of a dozen dead oceans" (A Hard Rain's A-Gonna Fall).

Besides love songs, in "The Freewheelin' Bob Dylan" Bob tried the so called social poetry. He has always refused to be considered as the voice of his generation crying out for the lost rights and other social causes. If we want to believe him, we will have to accept that what he was doing on these so called protest songs was to try new poetic images: "How many roads must a man walk down / Before you call him a man? / Yes, 'n' how many seas must a white dove sail / Before she sleeps in the sand? / Yes, 'n' how many times must the cannonballs fly / Before they're forever banned? The answer, my friend, is blowin' in the wind / The answer is blowin' in the wind." (Blowing In The Wind). "Masters Of War" is also a good example of poetic and dramatic images: "I will follow your casket / In the pale afternoon / And I'll watch while you're lowered / Down to your deathbed / And I'll stand o'er your grave / 'Til I'm sure that you're dead", and so it is "Oxford Town": "Oxford Town, Oxford Town / Ev'rybody's got their heads bowed down / The sun don't shine above the ground / Ain't a-goin' down to Oxford Town." Besides that, he just writes about daily occurrences: "While riding on a train goin' west, / I fell asleep for to take my rest. / I dreamed a dream that made me sad, / concerning myself and the first few friends I had" (Bob Dylan's Dream). It seems that Dylan is again extending the line. He wrote that, probably because he knew "I Think I'll catch me a freight train, 'cause I'm feeling blue" (San Francisco Blues).

Besides all that, Dylan wrote some surrealistic images in this album: "I was feelin' kinda lonesome and blue / I needed somebody to talk to / So I called up the operator of time /Just to hear a voice of some kind / "When you hear the beep it will be three o'clock" / She said that for over an hour / And I hung up" (Talkin' World War III Blues), and, for instance, he tells us about Adam and Eve in a fun way: "I took her by the hand and my heart it was thumpin' / When she said, "Hey man, you crazy or sumpin' / You see what happened last time they started" (Talkin' World War III Blues). Something similar happens in "I Shall Be Free": "Well, the funniest woman I ever seen / Was the great-granddaughter of Mr. Clean / She takes about fifteen baths a day / Wants me to grow a cigar on my face / She's a little bit heavy!" It seems that surrealism style allows Dylan to look at known characters from a different perspective. We will come back to this idea when we talk about "Desolation Row".

—*The Times They Are A-Changin' (January 13, 1964)*

Love songs of this album are about separation. On one hand, love is desired; on the other, that love -if reached- never lasts too much and it ends up in separation. However, the protagonists of this love-story have got to keep moving down the road: "You're right from your side / I'm right from mine / We're both just one too many mornings / An' a thousand miles behind" (One Too Many Mornings). Probably referring to separation he writes "The ocean wild like an organ played" (Lay Down Your Weary Tune), which is connected to

"Is there something I can send you from across the sea / From the place that I'll be landing?" (Boots Of Spanish Leather), and "When you wake up in the mornin', baby, look inside your mirror / You know I won't be next to you, you know I won't be near" (Mama, You Been On My Mind), which is connected to the line "When your rooster crows at the break of dawn / Look out your window and I'll be gone" (Don't Think Twice, It's All Right). In Booths of Spanish Leather, Dylan underlines the desire of reaching love when it's already gone: "Oh, but if I had the stars from the darkest night / And the diamonds from the deepest ocean / I'd forsake them all for your sweet kiss / For that's all I'm wishin' to be ownin.'"

"Restless Farewell" is a reflexion on lost love while he goes down the road: "Oh ev'ry girl that ever I've touched / I did not do it harmfully / And ev'ry girl that ever I've hurt / I did not do it knowin'ly / But to remain as friends / And make amends / You need the time and stay behind / And since my feet are now fast / And point away from the past / I'll bid farewell and be down the line", which is probably connected to "We're both just one too many mornings / An' a thousand miles behind" (One Too Many Mornings).

Other connexion we have found in this album is: "Come gather 'round people where ever you roam" (The Times They Are A-Changing), which extends the line "Gather 'round, people / A story I will tell" (Pretty Boy Floyd).

—Another Side of Bob Dylan (August 8, 1964)

There's a technique Dylan explores to write about love. We refer to narrative poems on which Dylan tells us about a failing love-story where the characters are alive like in a play. "Motorpsycho Nightmare" is a good example of this. Again, we don't think the point is to find out whether the story we are told in that song happened really to Dylan or not. It's about the construction of a narrative poem. Someone arrives at a farm: "I pounded on a farmhouse / Lookin' for a place to stay / I was mighty, mighty tired / I had come a long, long way" (Motorpsycho Nightmare). Then he falls in love with the daughter of the farmer: "Then in comes his daughter / Whose name was Rita / She looked like she stepped out of / La Dolce Vita". But things don't work out and he keeps going down the road: "The sun was comin' up/ And I was runnin' down the road" (Motorpsycho Nightmare). Again, it's not about trying to know whether Dylan lived this adventure in real world or not; rather it's about poetry: this is a narrative poem about a love story with some characters who interact on it. It's a combination of theatre, prose and poetry; and again Dylan is extending the line. He wrote "I had come a long, long way" (Motorpsycho Nightmare), which extends the line "I'm a long time a-comin' / An' I'll be a long time gone" (Long Time Gone), and he wrote "The sun was comin' up/ And I was runnin' down the road" (Motorpsycho Nightmare), which extends lines like "I'm goin' down to New Orleans, baby, behind the rising sun" (Going Down To New Orleans).

There are other connexions in this album. Although "Ballad in Plain D" refers to a specific Bob Dylan's love story that took place in the real world, as Howard Sounes points out (Sounes, 2011:163),

15

he repeats the poetic patterns he follows in other songs. Probably because he wrote "Look out your window and I'll be gone" (Don't Think Twice It's All Right), now he writes "I courted her proudly but now she is gone / Gone as the season she's taken"; and he talks about a window that is witness again to the end of a love story: "The wind knocks my window, the room it is wet / The words to say I'm sorry, I haven't found yet" (Ballad in Plain D).

In "It ain't me, babe!" Dylan starts off by taking up the line "The wind knocks my window, the room it is wet" (Ballad in Plain D) and saying: "Go 'way from my window / Leave at your own chosen speed / I'm not the one you want, babe / I'm not the one you need (It Ain't Me, Babe).

Dylan writes also "Crimson flames tied through my ears / Rollin' high and mighty traps / Pounced with fire on flaming roads / Using ideas as my maps / "We'll meet on edges, soon," said I" (My Back pages), and we will come back to these lines when Dylan extends them in later albums.

—*Bringing It All Back Home (March 22, 1965)*

In this album Dylan extends the line. He wrote "I ain't gonna work on Maggie's farm no more" (Maggie's Farm), probably because he knew that old tune: "I ain't gonna work on the railroad / I ain't gonna work on the farm / I'll roll in my sweet baby's arms" (Roll In My Sweet Baby's Arms), and then he came up with a new development in a different direction: "Well, I try my best / To be just like I am, / But everybody wants you / To be just like them" (Maggie's Farm).

Besides that, Dylan extends his own lines. He writes "My love she's like some raven / At my window with a broken wing" (Love Minus Zero, No Limit), because he wrote "The wind knocks my window, the room it is wet / The words to say I'm sorry, I haven't found yet", and because he wrote "Black crows in the meadow / Sleeping across a broad highway" (Black Crow Blues). He's again speaking of love using the same images he did in previous albums. Again, as he did in Don't Think Twice, It's All Right, Dylan focusses now on the moment of the separation: "You must leave now, take what you need, you think will last / But whatever you wish to keep, you better grab it fast" (It's All Over Now Baby Blue); and "The highway is for gamblers, better use your sense / Take what you have gathered from coincidence." (It's All Over Now Baby Blue). He writes "The lover who just walked out your door / Has taken all his blankets from the floor" (It's All Over Now, Baby Blue), because he wrote: "From the crossroads of my doorstep, / My eyes start to fade. / And I turn my head back to the room / Where my love and I have laid" (One Too Many Mornings). Now it's over, but he will try again: "Strike another match, go start anew" (It's All Over Now, Baby Blue).

The same way several tunes of this album meant the beginning of the change on Dylan's music style, several lyrics of this album worked out a new spin on Dylan's way of writing poetry. Songs like "Subterranean Homesick Blues", "Maggie's' Farm", "Outlaw Blues", "On The Road Again" and "Bob Dylan's 115th Dream" worked out a new music style, the so called folk-rock. In this album, Dylan started to write new images on his love songs. So to speak, "Bringing It All Back Home" is an album in which Dylan comes up with innovation in his verses, after having been extending the line in previous albums. Here are some of them: "She can take

17

the dark out of the night time / And paint the daytime black" (She Belongs to Me); "My love she speaks like silence" and "My love she speaks softly / She knows there's no success like failure / And that failure's no success at all" (Love Minus Zero, No Limit); "I got a woman in Jackson / I ain't gonna say her name / She's a brown-skin woman, / but I Love her just the same (Outlaw Blues). In "On the Road Again", love is impossible, because the family of the lover is impossible: "Then you ask why I don't live here / Honey, do you have to ask? / Honey, how come you have to ask me that? / Honey, I gotta think you're really weird / Honey, I can't believe that you're for real / Honey, how come you don't move?" Finally, love becomes a dream: "At dawn my lover comes to me / And tells me of her dreams / With no attempts to shovel the glimpse / Into the ditch of what each one means" (Gates of Eden). We will come back later to these images and their connexions with other verses.

In the context of an innovative poetry, it's relevant to point out that there's surrealistic poetry in "Bringing It All Back Home": "My love she laughs like the flowers" (Love Minus Zero / No Limit); "Ain't it hard to stumble / And land in some muddy lagoon? / Especially when it's nine below zero / And three o'clock in the afternoon" (Outlaw Blues); "Ain't gonna hang no picture, / Ain't gonna hang no picture frame. / Well, I might look like Robert Ford / But I feel just like a Jesse James" (Outlaw Blues); "I got my dark sunglasses, / I'm carryin' for good luck my black tooth. / Don't ask me nothin' about nothin', / I just might tell you the truth" (Out law Blues); "Well, I wake up in the morning / There's frogs inside my socks" (On The Road Again); "Your daddy walks in wearin' / A Napoleon Bonaparte mask" (On The Road Again); "I ask who's in the fireplace / And you tell me Santa Claus" (On The Road Again), just to

18

point out some examples. We will come back later to some of these verses that will be linked to new ones in following albums.

Before moving on to the next album, it's relevant to point out that Dylan keeps on bringing up to his songs known characters, as he did in "Freewheelin' Bob Dylan" (Adam and Eve in Talkin' World War III Blues.) Now, he talks about Robert Ford, Jesse James, Napoleon Bonaparte and Santa Claus. We will go back to this point later when we talk about "Desolation Row".

—*Highway 61 Revisited (August 30, 1965)*

In this album Dylan is again talking about looking for love: "Won't you come see me, Queen Jane?" (Queen Jane Approximately). He writes verses like "Well, I wanna be your lover, baby / I don't wanna be your boss" (It Takes A Lot To Laugh, It Takes A Train To Cry); and he states again that love could be impossible when he writes: "Well, I've been up all night, baby / Leanin' on the windowsill / Well, if I die / On top of the hill / And if I don't make it / You know my baby will" (It Takes A Lot To Laugh, It Takes A Train To Cry), and when he writes "Well, if I go down dyin', you know she bound to put a blanket on my bed" (From A Buick 6). We will come back to some of these lines, because Dylan extended them in future albums.

In this album we also notice a big step forward in the way Dylan writes poetry. "Desolation Row" is a good example. This song is about reinventing literary tradition into a something new. "The circus is in town" (Desolation Row), Dylan says. Then he stars mentioning known characters that belong to "Desolation Row". For

19

instance, Cinderella (who is compared to Bette Davis) interacts with Romeo; then, Dylan mentions Cain and Abel, the hunchback of Notre Dame and the Good Samaritan; then, Ophelia with an iron vest stares at Noah's rainbow from a window; then Einstein is compared to Robin Hood; then Dr. Filth, Casanova, the Phantom of the Opera are also mentioned; and finally Nero's Neptune, Titanic, Ezra Pound and T. S. Eliot. The last verse is important to figure out what Dylan is writing about. Speaking of the characters of Desolation Row, he says "I had to rearrange their faces / And give them all another name" (Desolation Row). This makes us bring up to consideration that Dylan is reinventing literary tradition through his poetry, and more specifically through his surrealistic poetry. At this point of his career Dylan has created —so to speak— his own world of people and thinks, as Woody Guthrie did from anonymous characters. Dylan knew very well that world as he wrote in Song To Woody: "I'm seeing your world of people and things / Hear paupers and peasants and princes and kings." Now Dylan is creating his own literary world from known characters that he reinvents. Cinderella is like Bette Davis, that's a good example. If Cinderella is like Bette Davis, then Dylan is deleting the border between reality and literature. He is turning reality into literature, into poetry. That's probably why "Desolation Row" is one of the master pieces ever written by Bob Dylan in an album that shows a mature Dylan as musician, performing artist and poet. As we have already pointed out, "Desolation Row" is the result of a long process that goes back —at least— to "Talkin' World War III Blues". The song Highway 61 Revisited is also a manifestation of that process: "Well Abe says, "Where do you want this killin' done?" / God says, "Out on Highway 61". We think that the petit maturity of this song is the result of a process in which Dylan extends the lines he wrote in "Talkin' World War III Blues" and "On The Road Again".

An important song of this album is "Like A Rolling Stone", and this song is also a good example of Dylan extending his own lines. He writes "How does it feel / To be on your own / With no direction home / like a complete unknown" (Like A Rolling Stone), probably because he wrote "I'm ready to go anywhere, I'm ready for to fade / Into my own parade (Mr. Tambourine Man), and probably because he wrote: "You lose yourself, you reappear / You suddenly find you got nothing to fear / Alone you stand with nobody near" (It's All Right Ma, I'm only Bleeding). And because he wrote that, he writes now "When you got nothing, you got nothing to lose / You're invisible now, you got no secrets to conceal" (Like A Rolling Stone). Dylan has reached one of the highest points in his career as a musician, performing artist and poet. However, there's a question that arises: What's he referring to? We will come back to this point, because Dylan extended some of these lines in future albums.

—*Playboy Interview (February 1966)*

Pretending to get some biographic information about Dylan from his answers in this interview would make no sense. This interview is not a source of information about Dylan's life. Reading Dylan's answers in this interview in that context would lead us nowhere. Rather, this interview is a great performance and a great sign of Dylan's productivity as a poet. It was not the first time Dylan was telling pretty —or not that pretty— stories about his life and the places he was living in, etc. He addressed to Izzy Young who was running The Folk Centre in New York that kind of discourse. During this interview on Dylan's mind was probably the idea of Woody Guthrie touring the US.

Some answers given by Dylan in the *Playboy* interview show that he's once again performing; this time he was extending the line from old tunes that have been always on the back of his mind inspiring him. When he was asked about what made him decide to go to rock 'n' roll route he said "I lost my one true love", probably because he knew that old tune "got in trouble had to roam, left my gal and left my home, I heard that lonesome whistle blow"; he said "I'm in a card game, then I am in a crap game" probably because he knew Hank Williams' line "just a deck of cards and a jug of wine, and a woman's lies makes a life like mine, oh the day we met, I went astray I started rolling down that lost highway"; he said that he was rumbling around in the States (Phoenix, Philadelphia, Dallas, Omaha) getting different jobs probably because he knew that old tune "Lord, I was born a ramblin' man, tryin' to make a livin' and doin' the best I can". He said that someone "burnt his house down", probably because he knew "Rocky Mountain Belle", Ramblin Jack Elliot (1959) "oh, they're burning down the house I was brung up in, and they're shouting come on out and take your bride"; he said that he "hit the road" probably because he knew Woody Guthrie's old tune "I'm going to hit that Oregon trial this coming fall". And so on.

—*Blonde On Blonde (May 16, 1966)*

Dylan started moving forward from folk music to rock music in "Bringing It All Back Home" and "Highway 61 Revisited". As meany critics have pointed out, Dylan created folk-rock music and gave us those two albums on that style. We have seen that his lyrics also progressed to the extent of creating new images. So, "Blonde On Blonde" means the steadiness on that change not only from the point of view of his music, but also his lyrics. In "Blonde on Blonde" Dylan has given us beautiful folk-rock songs (for instance, "Visions Of Johanna"), and rhythm and blues songs ("Obviously Five Believers", "Leopard-Skin Pill-Box Hat", "Pledging My Time"), just to point out some of the styles that are present in this album and a few of the most relevant titles of this album.

Regarding the lyrics of "Blonde On Blonde", Dylan starts off this album writing about his success and about the fact that many people didn't understand: "Well, they'll stone ya when you're trying to be so good"; "Well, they'll stone ya when you're walkin' 'long the street"; "They'll stone ya when you are young and able"; "Well, they'll stone you and say that it's the end"; "Well, they'll stone you when you walk all alone / They'll stone you when you are walking home". Then Dylan says that he couldn't care less about these criticisms: "I would not feel so all alone, everybody must get stoned" (Rainy Day Women #12 & 35)

Then, he writes about the difficulties that love faces and the difficulties to succeed in love: Won't you come with me, baby? / I'll take you where you wanna go / And if it don't work out / You'll be the first to know / I'm pledging my time to you / Hopin' you'll come through, too" (Pledging My Time). Sometimes Dylan keeps on extending his own lines: "After he stole my baby, then he wanted to steal me" (Pledging My Time) probably extends the line "well, the ocean took my baby, / My baby stole my heart from me" (Down The Highway).

In some songs of this album, love doesn't work out, for instance, "4th Time Around": "She threw me outside, / I stood in the dirt where ev'ryone walked. / And after finding I'd / Forgotten my shirt, / I went back and knocked." "One of Us Must Know (Sooner Or Later)" is also about that: "But, sooner or later, one of us must know, / You just did what you're supposed to do, / Sooner or later, one of us must know, / That I really did try to get close to you". Then Dylan says "And then you told me later, as I apologized, / That you were just kiddin' me, you weren't really from the farm". What doest it mean "you weren't really from the farm"? In order to figure it out we can consider that probably Dylan extends the line "I pounded on a farmhouse / Lookin' for a place to stay"; and "Then in comes his daughter / Whose name was Rita", and "I immediately tried to cool it / With her dad / And told him what a / Nice, pretty farm he had" (Motorpsycho Nightmare), where a farm is a place where love-stories take place. Then Dylan says "I didn't mean to make you so sad" and "An' I told you, as you clawed out my eyes / That I never really meant to do you any harm" (One Of Us Must Know, Sooner Or Later), that extends the line "Oh ev'ry girl that ever I've touched / I did not do it harmfully / And ev'ry girl that ever I've hurt / I did not do it knowin'ly" (Restless Farewell). "Just Like a woman" tells a love-story that doesn't work out: "I just don't fit / Yes, I believe it's time for us to quit / And when we meet again / Introduced as friends / Please don't let on that you knew me when / I was hungry and it was your world." In "Most Likely You Go Your Way I'll Go Mine" love doesn't work out either: "I'm just gonna let you pass, / Yes, and I'll go last. / Then time will tell who fell / And who's been left behind, / When you go your way and I go mine."

Dylan writes about the lover who tries to fight for his love by using simple images: "I wasn't born to lose you. / I want you, I want you, / I want you so bad, / Honey, I want you" (I Want You); but also by using surrealistic images: "You know it balances on your head / Just like a mattress balances / On a bottle of wine / Your brand new leopard-skin pill-box hat"; "Well, if you wanna see the sun rise / Honey, I know where / We'll go out and see it sometime / We'll both just sit there and stare / Me with my belt Wrapped around my head / And you just sittin' there (Leopard-Skin Pill-Box Hat). In "Obviously 5 Believers" the lover calls for love, but in a different way: "Early in the mornin' / I'm callin' you to / Please come home" (Obviously 5 Believers), that extends the line "I see the morning light / I see the morning light / Well, it's not because / I'm an early riser / I didn't go to sleep last night" (Walkin' Down The Line). And he the lover wants to fight: "Don't let me down / I won't let you down / I won't let you down / No I won't" (Obviously 5 Believers). In "Absolutely Sweet Marie" Dylan calls the lover "where are you tonight, sweet Marie?"; but the love story doesn't have a happy end: "Well, six white horses that you did promise / Were fin'lly delivered down to the penitentiary / But to live outside the law, you must be honest / I know you always say that you agree". This love story doesn't work, because he's the bad guy, the outlaw, "just another guy on the lost highway" (Lost Highway), who lives outside the law following his own rules, rules that she doesn't accept, then, the love story doesn't work, thats probably why Dylan sings "but where are you tonight, sweet Marie?"

In "Temporary Like Aquilles", Dylan extends his own lines. He writes "Standing on your window, honey, / Yes, I've been here before" because he wrote "Look out your window and I'll be gone /

You're the reason I'm trav'lin' on" (Dont Think Twice). Of course, he has been there before: "My love she's like some raven / At my window with a broken wing" (Love Minus Zero, No Limit); "The wind knocks my window (Black Crow Blues). "Temporary Like Aquilles" is not going to be the last time we see the lover at a window talking about love: "Down over the window / Come the dazzling sunlit rays / Through the back alleys, through the blinds, / Another one of them endless days" (Floater, Too Much To Ask).

Dylan writes "And Louise holds a handful of rain, temptin' you to defy it" (Visions Of Johanna), which is probably connected to "And it's a hard rain's a-gonna fall" (A Hard Rain's A-Gonna Fall). He writes "And the all-night girls they whisper of escapades out on the "D" train" (Visions Of Johanna), which is connected to "Well, I ride on a mailtrain, baby / Can't buy a thrill / Well, I've been up all night, baby / Leanin' on the windowsill" (It Takes A Lot To Laugh, It Takes A Train To Cry). Dylan writes "The harmonicas play the skeleton keys and the rain / And these visions of Johanna are now all that remain" (Visions Of Johanna), which is probably linked to "I'm a-goin' back out 'fore the rain starts a-fallin'" (A Hard Rain's A-Gonna Fall).

—*John Wesley Harding (December 27, 1967)*

Once and again, Dylan is grounded in folk tradition. John Wesley Harding is a "come all you song" and Dylan writes "'Twas down in Chaynee County, / A time they talk about, / With his lady by his side / He took a stand," probably because he sang "It was in the town of Shawnee / A Saturday afternoon, / his wife beside him in his wagon / As into town they rode" (Pretty Boy Floyd). Again, Dylan writes "let me just warn you all, / Before I do pass on; / Stay free from petty jealousies, / Live by no man's code, / And hold your judgment for yourself / Lest you wind up on this road" (I Am A Lonesome Hobo), because, again, he sang "now boys don't start to ramblin' round / on this road of sin are you sorrow bound / take my advice or you'll curse the day / you started rollin' down that lost highway." (Lost Highway).

Dylan extends his own lines too in this album. He wrote "I offer'd her my hand / She took me by the arm / I knew that very instant / She meant to do me harm" (As I Went Out One Morning), which extends the line "I give her my heart but she wanted my soul" (Don't Think Twice It's All Right), because in both lines he's pointing out the fact that in a love story she can ask for too much and that could be the beginning of the end of that love-story.

In this album Dylan comes up with innovation in "All Along The Watchtower": "There must be some way out of here," said the joker to the thief / "There's too much confusion, I can't get no relief / Businessmen, they drink my wine, plowmen dig my earth / None of them along the line know what any of it is worth." We will come back to some of these lines, because Dylan extended them in future albums.

—*Nashville Skyline (April 9, 1969)*

Love: that's what everything is all about: "Love is all there is, it makes the world go 'round, / Love and only love, it can't be denied. / No matter what you think about it / You just won't be able to do without it. / Take a tip from one who's tried (I Threw It All

Away). But love doesn't last too long. Dylan writes "I can hear that lonesome whistle blowin' / I hear them semis rolling too / If there's a driver on the road / let him have my load / cause tonight I'll be staying here with you", because he sang I'll never see that girl of mine, / for I'm in Georgia doing time, / I heard that lonesome whistle blow" (Lonesome Whistle Blues). And he writes "Stay, lady, stay, stay with your man awhile/ Until the break of day" (Lay, Lady, Lay), probably because he wrote "when your rooster crows at the break of dawn / look out your window and I'll be gone" (Don't Think Twice It's All Right).

The idea of love as something impossible is back on this album. Dylan writes "I just could not be what she wanted me to be" (One More Night), probably because he sang "she wants me to be a hero" (Hero Blues), and because he wrote "I'm not the one you want, babe, I'm not the one you need" (It Ain't Me, Babe).

—*Self Portrait (1970)*

Dylan writes "Oh my heart is so sad / Cause I want you so bad / Alberta don't you treat me unkind" (Alberta), which is connected to "I want you, I want you, / I want you so bad, / Honey, I want you" (I Want You).

Dylan sings "I'm a long way from home and I miss my love one so / In the early morning rain with nowhere to go" (Early Mornin' Rain), because he wrote "Oh I miss my darling so" (One More Night).

Dylan writes "Well they took me down town and they dressed me in black, / They put me on a train and they sent me back / They crammed me back into the county jail /   Forty-one years to wear the ball and the stripes" (In Search Of Little Sadie), because he sang "They took me off the Georgia Main / Locked me to a ball and chain / I heard that lonesome whistle blow" (Lonesome Whistle Blues).

Sometimes, Dylan draws the setting of a love-scene in nature: One evenin' for pleasure / I rambled to view the fair fields all alone / Down by the banks of Loch Erin / Where beauty an' pleasure were known / I spied a fair maid at her labor / Which caused me to stay for a while / An' I thought of a goddess of beauty / Bloomin' bright star of Bright Isle. / I humbled myself to her beauty / "Fair maiden where do you belong? / Are you from heaven descended / Abidin' in Cupid's fair throne." (Belle Isle)

He sings "There's a lonesome freight at 6:08 coming through the town, / And I feel like I just want to travel on" (Gotta Travel On), because he wrote "when the whistle blows I gotta go baby, / Well, it looks like I'm never gonna lose the freight train blues" (Freight Train Blues).

He sings "I don't wanna be your boss babe, i just wanna be your man" (It Hurts Me Too), because he wrote "Well, I wanna be your lover, baby / I don't wanna be your boss" (It Takes A Lot To Laugh, It Takes A Train To Cry).

—*New Morning (1970)*

Dylan writes again about the difficulties of love by referring to "a window": "Sign on the window says "Lonely," / Sign on the door said "No Company Allowed," / Sign on the street says "Y' Don't Own Me,"" (Sign On The Window), which extends some lines we have quoted before. This time he seems more optimistic: "Once I had a sweetheart, / Starin' out the window to the stars high above, / Time passes slowly when you're searchin' for love" (Time Passes Slowly). Dylan wrote "when your rooster crows at the break of dawn / Look out your window and I'll be gone" (Don't think twice) and now he writes "Can't you hear that rooster crowin'? / So happy just to see you smile / Underneath the sky of blue / On this new morning with you" (New Morning), which probably means that the protagonist of the love-story in "New Morning" know that things are not going to last too much.

He writes "Like a needle in a haystack, I'm gonna find you yet, / You're the sweetest gone mama that this boy's ever gonna get" (One More Weekend), which is connected to "Well, lookin' for a woman / That ain't got no man / Is just lookin' for a needle / That is lost in the sand" (Honey Just Allow Me One More Chance), probably meaning in general difficulties in love.

We will come back to lines like "Storm clouds are raging all around my door, / I think to myself I might not take it any more (The Man In Me), because Dylan extends them in albums to come.

30

—*Dylan (A Fool As Such I)*

He sings "An' I am bound away for the sea" (Mary Ann), because he wrote "Well, the ocean took my baby / My baby stole my heart from me" (Down The Highway).

—*Planet Waves (1974)*

In this album, Dylan recorded one his most beautiful songs: "Forever Young". We think that what really matters is what Dylan was thinking of when he wrote this song and dedicated it to one of his sons. The fact that he is referring to his son Jacob or not is not the most relevant point. Again, the relevant point is to figure out up to what extent Dylan was extending lines and which ones when he wrote this song. That's going to give us the real background to understand what he was probably thinking of when he wrote it. He wrote "May you build a ladder to the stars / And climb on every rung" (Forever Young), which is connected to "I saw a white ladder all covered with water" (A Hard Rain's A Gonna Fall). He wrote "May your hands always be busy / May your feet always be swift" (Forever Young), which extends the line "And since my feet are now fast / And point away from the past / I'll bid farewell and be down the line" (Restless Farewell). He wrote "May your heart always be joyful / And may your song always be sung / May you stay forever young" (Forever Young), which is connected to "The tune that is yours and mine to play upon this earth / We'll play it out the best we know, whatever it is worth" (Wedding Song).

Beside, Dylan writes about lost love: "Build me a cabin in Utah, / Marry me a wife, catch rainbow trout, / Have a bunch of kids who call me "Pa," / That must be what it's all about", which extends the line "Wishin' my long-lost lover / Will walk to me, talk to me / Tell me what it's all about" (Black Crow Blues). He writes "Twilight on the frozen lake / North wind about to break / On footprints in the snow / Silence down below" (Never Say Goodbye), which is connected to "Well, if you're travelin' in the north country fair / Where the winds hit heavy on the borderline / Well, if you go when the snowflakes storm/ When the rivers freeze and summer ends" (Girl From The North Country).

In this album Dylan says something new and original about the lover: Dylan writes "Sweet Goddess / Born of a blinding light and a changing wind, / Now, don't be modest, / you know who you are and where you've been" (Tough Mama), which is connected to "Oh, where have you been, my blue-eyed son? / Oh, where have you been, my darling young one?" (A Hard Rain's A-Gonna Fall). We will come back to these lines later, when we deal with some extensions of them Dylan wrote in later albums.

—*Blood On The Tracks (1975)*

Dylan writes "Early one mornin' the sun was shinin', / he was layin' in bed / Wond'rin' if she'd changed at all / If her hair was still red" (Tangle up in blue) which extends the line "Early in the mornin' / I'm callin' you to / Please come home" (Obviously Five Believers). He writes the line "tangle up in blue", that extends the line "It's all over now baby blue" (It's All Over Now, Baby Blue). Love is red when it's still possible; love is blue when it's gone. Dylan writes "And he was standin' on the side of the road / Rain fallin' on his shoes" (Tangled up in blue), which extends the line "Right now I'm havin' trouble / Please don't take away my highway shoes" (Down The Highway). Dylan writes "We always did feel the same, / We just saw it from a different point of view" (Tangle Up In Blue), which extends lines like " You're right from your side / I'm right from mine / We're both just one too many mornings / An' a thousand miles behind (One Too Many Mornings). Dylan writes "Our conversation was short and sweet / It nearly swept me off-a my feet. / And I'm back in the rain, oh / And you are on dry land" (You're A Big Girl Now), which is connected to "And he was standin' on the side of the road / Rain fallin' on his shoes" (Tangled up in blue).

Dylan writes "They sat together in the park / As the evening sky grew dark" (Simple Twist Of Fate), that means that the landscape of a love-story is dark and cloudy. Again he writes about the window: "He woke up, the room was bare / He didn't see her anywhere. / He told himself he didn't care, / pushed the window open wide" (Simple Twist Of Fate).

And he writes "Bird on the horizon, sittin' on a fence, He's singin' his song for me at his own expense / And I'm just like that bird, oh, oh,/ Singin' just for you, mm-mm / I hope that you can hear, / Hear me singin' through these tears" (You're A Big Girl Now), which extends the line "I got a bird that whistles / I got a bird that sings / But I ain' a-got Corrina / Life don't mean a thing (Corrina, Corrina).

Dylan writes "I've seen love go by my door / It's never been this close before / Never been so easy or so slow" (You're Gonna Make Me Lonesome When You Go) which is related to "Highway 51

33

runs right by my baby's door" (Highway 51), and others lyrics talking about the door if the house of the lover.

"They say the darkest hour is right before the dawn / Little rooster crowin', there must be something on his mind / Well, I feel just like that rooster / Honey, ya treat me so unkind" (Meet Me In The Morning), which extends the line "When your rooster crows at the break of dawn / Look out your window and I'll be gone" (Don't Think Twice It's All Right).

"The next day was hangin' day, the sky was overcast and black, / Big Jim lay covered up, killed by a penknife in the back" (Lily, Rosemary and the Jack of Hearts) that extends the line "your grass is turning black / there's no water in your well / There's seven people dead / On a South Dakota farm" (Ballad Of Hollis Brown), where black is the sign of a close death.

Dylan writes "I came in from the wilderness, a creature void of form. / "Come in," she said, "I'll give you shelter from the storm" (Shelter From The Storm) which probably extends the line "And I'm back in the rain, oh / And you are on dry land" (You're A Big Girl Now), and also "You're invisible now, you got no secrets to conceal" (Like A Rolling Stone) and "I'm ready to go anywhere, I'm ready for to fade / Into my own parade, cast your dancing spell my way / I promise to go under it" (Mr Tambourine Man). Precisely because the lover is a creature void of form, he's also invisible, and fades.

Dylan writes "And if we never meet again, baby, remember me, / How my lone guitar played sweet for you that old-time melody

(Up To Me) which extends the line "I sang the song slowly / As she stood in the shadows" (Eternal Circle).

—*The Basement Tapes (1975)*

Dylan writes "This wheel's on fire / Rolling down the road / Best notify my next of kin / This wheel shall explode!" (This Wheel's On Fire), which extends among others the line "Well, I'm a-walkin' down the road / With my head in my hand / I'm lookin' for a woman / Needs a worried man" (Honey Just Allow Me One More Chance).

Dylan writes "I'm just goin' down the road t' see Bessie / Oh, see her soon / Goin' down the road t' see Bessie Smith / When I get there I wonder what she"l do" (Bessie Smith), which extends the line "Slippin' and slidin' like a weasel on the run / I'm lookin' good to see you, yeah, and we can have some fun" (One More Weekend).

Dylan writes "Oh, Katie, if you can hear me, / I just can't wait to have you near me. I can only think / Where are you, / What ya do, may be there's someone new" (Katie' Been Gone), which is connected to "Early in the mornin' / I'm callin' you to / Please come home / Yes, I guess I could make it without you / If I just didn't feel so all alone" (Obviously Five Believers).

He writes "Well, that high tide's risin' / Mama, don't you let me down / Pack up your suitcase / Mama, don't you make a sound (Crash On The Levee, Down In The Flood), which is connected to "She packed it all up in a suitcase / Lord, she took it away to Italy, Italy" (Down The Highway)

—*Desire (1976)*

      Dylan writes "I rode straight away / for the wild unknown country where I could not go wrong" (Isis), which is connected to "I came in from the wilderness, a creature void of form" (Shelter From The Storm). He writes "Not a word was spoke between us, there was little risk involved / Everything up to that point had been left unresolved" (Shelter From The Storm), which extends the line "Still I wish there was somethin' you would do or say / To try and make me change my mind and stay / We never did too much talkin' anyway" (Don't Think Twice It's All Right) and the line "My love she speaks like silence / my love she speaks softly" (Love Minus Zero/No Limit).

      He writes "One more cup of coffee 'fore I go / To the valley below" (One More Cup Of Coffee, Valley Below), which extends the line "I walked down to the valley" (Paths Of Victory), which extends the line "Where the home in the valley meets the damp dirty prison" (A Hard Rain's A Gonna Fall).

      He writes "Oh, sister, when I come to knock on your door / Don't turn away, you'll create sorrow" (Oh, Sister), which is connected to "Don't let me down" (Obviously Five Believers).

      Dylan writes "Time is an ocean but it ends at the shore" (Oh, Sister), which extends the line "Why am I walking, where am I running / What am I saying, what am I knowing / In this ocean of hours I'm all the time drinkin'" (Last Thoughts on Woody Guthrie). Those lines are connected to "Time is piling up, we struggle and we scrape. / We're all boxed in, nowhere to escape" (Mississippi).

He writes "The way is long but the end is near" (Romance In Durango), which extends the line "But the good road is a-waiting / And boys it ain't far off" (Paths of Victory).

He writes "How did I meet you? I don't know. / A messenger sent me in a tropical storm. / You were there in the winter, moonlight on the snow / And on Lily Pond Lane when the weather was warm" (Sara), that extends the line "Come in," she said, "I'll give you shelter from the storm".

—*Street legal (1978)*

Dylan writes "It was early in the mornin', I seen your shadow in the door / Now, I don't have to ask nobody / I know what you come here for" (New Pony) once again Dylan places the love story at a door, like in "Señor, señor, do you know where she is hidin'? / How long are we gonna be ridin'? / How long must I keep my eyes glued to the door? / Will there be any comfort there, señor?" (Senor, Tales Of Yankee Power).

He wrote "You know you can't keep her and the water gets deeper / That is leading you onto the brink" (No time to think), which probably extends the line "Well, that high tide's risin' / Mama, don't you let me down" (Crash On The Levee, Down In The Flood) and "you better start swimming or you will sink like a stone" (The Times They Are A-Changin').

37

"No time to think" extends the line "You might see me on your crossroads / When I'm a-passin' through / Remember me how you wished to / As I'm a-driftin' from your view / I ain't got the time to think about it / I got too much to get done" (Long time gone).

"Go down to the river, babe / Honey, I will meet you there / Go down to the river, babe / Honey, I will pay your fare" (Baby Stop Crying) extends the line "I walked down by the river / I turned my head up high / I saw that silver linin' / That was hangin' in the sky / Trails of troubles / Roads of battles" (Paths Of Victory).

Dylan writes about the way the lover is. He writes "Señor, señor, you know their hearts is as hard as leather" (Senor, Tales Of Yankee Power) which extends the line "And yes, there's something you can send back to me / Spanish boots of Spanish leather" (Boots of Spanish Leather). He writes "When she's near me she's so hard to recognize" (True Love Tends To Forget), which extends the line "so easy to look at, so hard to define" (Sara).

He writes "I saw you in the wilderness among the men" (True Love Tends to Forget), which extends the line "I came in from the wilderness, a creature void of form" (Shelter From the Storm).

He writes "Let's call it a day, go our own different ways" (We Better Talk This Over), which extends the line "You're right from your side / I'm right from mine" (One Too Many Mornings) and "When you go your way and I go mine" (Most Likely You Go Your Way And I'll Go Mine). He writes "I guess I'll be leaving

38

tomorrow" (We Better Talk This Over) which extends the line "I'm leaving tomorrow but I could leave today" (Song To Woody).

He writes "There's a long-distance train rolling through the rain / Tears on the letter I write" (Where Are You Tonight? Journey Through Dark Heat), and "There's a new day at dawn and I've finally arrived / If I'm there in the morning, baby, you'll know I've survived" (Where Are You Tonight? Journey Through Dark Heat), which extends the line "Well, I ride on a mailtrain, baby / Can't buy a thrill / Well, I've been up all night, baby / Leanin' on the windowsill / Well, if I die / On top of the hill / And if I don't make it / You know my baby will" (It Takes A Lot To Laugh, It Takes A Train To Cry).

—Slow train coming (1979)

"Precious angel, under the sun / Shine your light, shine your light on me" (Precious Angel), and "You're the lamp of my soul, girl, and you torch up the night" (Precious Angel) extend the line "But tonight no light will shine on me" (One More Night); and "Ya know I just couldn't make it by myself" (Precious Angel) extends the line "Yes, I guess I could make it without you / If I just didn't feel so all alone" (Obviously Five Believers).

Dylan writes "They ask me how I feel / They'd like to drive me from this town / They don't want me around / And I walk out on my own / A thousand miles from home" (Slow Train Coming), which extends the following lines: "How does it feel / To be without a home / Like a complete unknown" (Like A Rolling Stone), and "I'm here a thousand miles from my home / walking a road other men have gone down" (Song To Woody).

Dylan writes "I don't care how rough the road is, show me where it starts" (What Can I Do For You), which extends the line "I was born very far from where I was supposed to be, so I'm on my way home!" (No Direction Home).

—*Shot Of Love (1981)*

He writes "I got the heart and you got the blood / We cut through iron and we cut through mud" (In Summertime), which extends the line "'Twas in another lifetime, one of toil and blood / When blackness was a virtue and the road was full of mud" (Shelter From the Storm).

—*Infidels (1983)*

Dylan writes "You know, I once knew a woman who looked like you / She wanted a whole man, not just a half" (Sweet Heart Like You), which extends the line "I give her my heart but she wanted my soul" (Don't Think Twice), and "I offer'd her my hand / She took me by the arm / I knew that very instant / She meant to do me harm" (As I Went Out One Morning).

Dylan writes: "Now, there's a woman on my block / She just sit there as the night grows still (License To Kill) which extends the line "We'll both just sit there and stare / Me with my belt / Wrapped around my head / And you just sittin' there / In your brand new leopard-skin pill-box hat" (Leopard-Skil Pill Box Hat).

Dylan writes "Look out your window, baby, there's a scene you'd like to catch / Somewhere Mama's weeping for her blue-eyed boy / She's holding them little white shoes and that little broken toy" (Man Of Peace), which extends the line "Oh, where have you been my blue-eyed son / Oh, where have you been, my darling young one?" (A Hard Rain's A-Gonna Fall).

—Empire Burlesque (1985)

Dylan writes "I'll go along with this charade / Until I can think my way out. / I know it was all a big joke / Whatever it was about (Tight Connexion To My Heart, Has Anybody Seen My Love), which extends the line "There must be some way out of here," said the joker to the thief / "There's too much confusion, I can't get no relief / "No reason to get excited," the thief, he kindly spoke / "There are many here among us who feel that life is but a joke (All Along The Watchtower).

He writes "You're the one I've been looking for, / You're the one that's got the key" (Tight Connexion To My Heart, Has Anybody Seen My Love), which extends the line "You gimme a map and a key to your door" (Sara).

"Never could learn to hold you, love / And call you mine" (Tight Connexion To My Heart, Has Anybody Seen My Love) extends the line "I married Isis on the fifth day of May / But I could not hold on to her very long" (Isis).

Dylan wrote "I'd like to get you to change your mind / But it looks like you won't / Whatever you gonna do / Please do it fast / I'm still trying to get used to / Seeing the real you at last" (Seeing The Real You At Last), which extends the line "You must leave now, take what you need, you think will last / But whatever you wish to keep, you better grab it fast" (It's All Over Now, Baby Blue).

I'll remember you / When the wind blows through the piney wood (I'll Remember You) extends the line "Where the winds hit heavy on the borderline" (Girl From The North Country) and the line "The winter wind is a blowing strong" (Kingsport Town).

"I'll remember you / At the end of the trail" (I'll Remember You) extends the line "Don't you remember me babe / I remember you quite well / You caused me to leave old Kingsport Town / With a high sheriff on my trail" (Kingsport Town).

Dylan sings "Come baby, find me, come baby, remind me of where I once begun" (Emotionally Yours), which, again, extends the following lines: "I don't care how rough the road is, show me where it starts" (What Can I Do For You), and "I was born very far from where I was supposed to be, so I'm on my way home!" (No Direction Home).

He writes "For all eternity I think I will remember / That icy wind that's howling in your eye" (When The Night Comes Falling From The Sky) which extends the line "The winter wind is a blowing strong / Who's a-gonna look you straight in the eye" (Kingsport Town).

"I know everything about this place, or so it seems / We've reached the edge of the road, baby, where the pasture begins" (Something's Burning, Baby) extends the line "I been walkin' the road, / I been livin' on the edge, / Now, I've just got to go / Before I get to the ledge" (Going, Going, Gone).

He writes "Oh, time is short and the days are sweet and passion rules the arrow that flies / A million faces at my feet but all I see are dark eyes" (Dark Eyes), which extends the line "I glanced at my guitar / And played it pretendin' / That of all the eyes out there / I could see none / As her thoughts pounded hard / Like the pierce of an arrow" (Eternal Circle).

—*Knocked Out Loaded (1986)*

In this album Dylan writes "I said Baby, I know where you been / Well, I know who you are / You wanna ramble / To the break of dawn" (You Wanna Ramble), which extends the line "When your rooster crows at the break of dawn" and "Oh, Where have you been my blue-eyed son" (A Hard Rain's A-Gonna Fall).

"I try to reach you honey / But you're driftin' too far from shore" (Driftin' Too Far from Shore) extends the line "the ocean took my baby" (Down The Highway) and "I'm sailin' away in the morning" (Boots Of Spanish Leather).

"As I travel down life's pathway / Know not what the years may hold / As I ponder hopes grow fonder / Precious memories flood my soul" (Precious Memories) extends the line "And as through this world I've rambled / I've seen lots of funny men; / Some will rob you with a six-gun, / And some with a fountain pen" (Pretty Boy Floyd).

—*Down In The Groove (1988)*

"When storm clouds gather round you / And heavy rains descend / Just remember that death is not the end (Death Is Not The End) extends the line "Then I'll stand on the ocean until I start sinkin' / But I'll know my song well before I start singin' / And it's a hard, it's a hard, it's a hard, it's a hard / It's a hard rain's a-gonna fall" (A Hard Rain's A-Gonna Fall) and the line "That long black cloud is comin' down / I feel like I'm knockin' on heaven's door" (Knocking On Heaven's Door).

"Standin' on the highway, you flag me down / Said, take me Daddy, to the nearest town / You got a rag wrapped around your head / Wearing a long dress fire engine red" (Had A Dream About You, Baby) extends the line "Me with my belt / Wrapped around my head / And you just sittin' there / In your brand new leopard-skin pill-box hat" (Leopard-Skin Pill-Box Hat) and the line "Early one mornin' the sun was shinin' / I was layin' in bed / Wond'rin' if she'd changed at all / If her hair was still red" (Tangled Up In Blue).

"When she says babababababy I l-l-love you / There ain't nothing in the world that I wouldn't do" (Ugliest girl) extends the line "Ah'll do anything with you / Well, I've been lookin' all over (Honey, Just Allow Me One More Chance).

"When I get low she sets me on my feet" (Ugliest Girl In The World) extends the line "You say you're lookin' for someone / Who'll pick you up each time you fall" (It Ain't Me, Babe).

44

"When I come knocking don't throw me no bone / I'm an old boll weevil looking for a home" (Silvio) is connected "Go away from my door and my window too / Right now" (Bob Dylan's Blues).

"One of these days and it won't be long / Going down in the valley and sing my song / I will sing it loud and sing it strong / Let the echo decide if I was right or wrong" (Silvio) extends the line "But I'll know my song well before I start singin'" (A Hard Rain's A-Gonna Fall) and other lines: "May your heart always be joyful / And may your song always be sung / May you stay forever young" (Forever Young), "The tune that is yours and mine to play upon this earth / We'll play it out the best we know, whatever it is worth" (Wedding Song), and "She breathed hard through the echo / But the song it was long / And it was far to the end / As the tune finally folded / I laid down the guitar / Then looked for the girl / Who'd stayed for so long / But her shadow was missin' / For all of my searchin' / So I picked up my guitar / And began the next song" (Eternal Circle).

—*Oh Mercy* (1989)

"Thinking of you when the sun comes up / Where teardrops fall" (Where Teardrops Fall) extends the line "Early one mornin' the sun was shinin' / I was layin' in bed / Wond'rin' if she'd changed at all / If her hair was still red" (Tangled Up In Blue).

Dylan writes "Crickets are chirpin', the water is high / There's a soft cotton dress on the line hangin' dry / Window wide open, African trees" (Man In The Long Black Coat), which extends the line "And admit that the waters / Around you have grown" (The Times They Are A-Changin') and "He told himself he didn't care, pushed the window open wide / Felt an emptiness inside to which he just could not relate" (Simple Twist Of Fate).

He writes "Bent over backwards from a hurricane breeze" (Man In The Long Black Coat), which extends several lines, for instance, "Where the winds hit heavy on the borderline" (Girl From The North Country). Dylan writes "Not a word of goodbye, not even a note / She gone with the man / In the long black coat" (Man In The Long Black Coat), which extends the line "We never did too much talkin' anyway" (Don't Think Twice It's All Right).

Dylan writes "I can keep both feet on the ground / I can follow the path, I can read the signs / I can handle whatever I stumble upon / I don't even notice she's gone" (Most Of The Time), which extends the line "Ain't it hard to stumble / And land in some funny lagoon?" (Outlaw Blues).

"What's happening in there / What's going on in your show" (What Was It You Wanted) extends the line "Still I wish there was somethin' you would do or say" (Don't Think Twice, It's All Right). Dylan writes "Are they playing our song?" (What Was It You Wanted), which extends the line "The tune that is yours and mine to play upon this earth / We'll play it out the best we know, whatever it is worth" (Wedding Song).

—*Under The Red Sky (1990)*

"Once there was a man who had no eyes / Every lady in the land told him lies / He stood beneath the silver sky and his heart began to bleed" (Unbelievable), probably extends the line "Mama, take this badge off of me / I can't use it anymore / It's gettin' dark, too dark for me to see / I feel like I'm knockin' on heaven's door" (Knocking On Heavens Door).

"Oh babe, that fire / Is still smokin' / You were snow, you were rain" (Born In Time) extends several lines, for instance, "The wind it was howlin' and the snow was outrageous / We chopped through the night and we chopped through the dawn" (Isis).

"God knows there's a river / God knows how to make it flow / God knows you ain't gonna be taking / Nothing with you when you go" (God Knows) extends the line "Let the bird sing, let the bird fly / One day the man in the moon went home and the river went dry" (Under The Red Sky).

"God knows you can rise above the darkest hour / Of any circumstance" (God Knows) extends the line "When storm clouds gather round you / And heavy rains descend / Just remember that death is not the end (Death Is Not The End).

—*Good As I Been To You (1992)*

"Oh, where is little Maggie / Over yonder she stands, / Rifle on her shoulder, / Six-shooter in her hand" (Little Maggie), extends the line I" saw guns and sharp swords in the hands of young children" (A Hard Rain's A-Gonna Fall) and the line "Frankie pulled out a pistol. / Pulled out a forty-four. / Gun went off a rootie-toot-toot" (Frankie & Albert).

"Pull off, pull off them high-heeled shoes / All made of Spanish leather" (Black Jack Davey) is connected to "And yes, there's something you can send back to me / Spanish boots of Spanish leather" (Boots of Spanish Leather).

"Oh, I'm sailin' away my own true love / I'm sailin' away in the morning" (Boots of Spanish leather) is connected to "She fell in love with a sailor boy" (Canadee-I-o). In Dylan's poetry sailors in love are related to distance between lovers, but this time things work out: "Now, when they come down to Canada / Scarcely 'bout half a year, / She's married this bold captain / Who called her his dear" (Canadee-i-o).

"Was in the summer, / One early fall / Was in the spring, / One summer's day. / Now she's gone / I'm sittin' on top of the world. / Went to the station, / Down in the yard, / Gonna get me a freight train" (Sittin' On Top Of The World) extends the line "I got the freight train blues / Oh Lord mama, I got them in the bottom of my rambling shoes / And when the whistle blows I gotta go baby, don't you know / Well, it looks like I'm never gonna lose the freight train blues" (Freight Train Blues).

Dylan writes "Well, it's march me away to the station / With my suitcase in my hand, / Yes, march me away to the station, / I'm off to some far-distant land" (Little Maggie), which extends the line "Yes, I'm walkin' down the highway / With my suitcase in my hand / Lord, I really miss my baby / She's in some far-off land" (Down The Highway).

"There's a song that will linger forever in our ears, / Oh, hard times, come again no more / 'Tis the song, the sigh of the weary. / Hard times, hard times, come again no more" (Hard Times) extends the line "Lay down your weary tune, lay down / Lay down the song you strum / And rest yourself 'neath the strength of strings / No voice can hope to hum" (Lay Down Your Weary Tune). Dylan writes "Tomorrow night, will it be just another memory / Or just another song, that's in my heart to linger on?" (Tomorrow Night), which extends the line "There's a song that will linger forever in our ears, / Oh, hard times, come again no more / 'Tis the song, the sigh of the weary (Hard Times) and the line "Lay down your weary tune, lay down / Lay down the song you strum" (Lay Down Your Weary Tune).

Why did Bob Dylan record "Froggie Went A-Courtin'? Probably because it's a traditional song about love, with the scenarios Dylan likes. Dylan sang "Took Miss Mousey on his knee. / Said, "Miss Mousey, will you marry me?" Uh-huh" (Froggie Went A-Courtin'), because he sang "Would you marry me, Pretty Peggy-O / Would you marry me, your cities I will free" (Pretty Peggy-O). Dylan sang "Well he rode up to Miss Mousey's door. / Gave three loud raps and a very big roar, Uh-huh" (Froggie Went A-Courtin'), because he sang "Highway 51 runs right by my baby's door / If I don't get the girl I'm loving / Won't go down to Highway 51 no more" (Highway 51) and because he sang "My warehouse eyes, my Arabian drums, / Should I put them by your gate, / Or, sad-eyed lady, should I wait?" (Sad Eyed Lady Of The Lowlands).

—*World Gone Wrong* (1993)

"He was just a blue-eyed Boston boy, / (...) There's no one to write to the blue-eyed girl / the words that her lover had said. / Momma, you know, awaits the news, / And she'll only know he's dead" (Two Soldiers) extends the line "Oh, what did you see, my blue-eyed son? / Oh, what did you see, my darling young one?" (A Hard Rain's A Gonna Fall).

"Now Jackie's gone sailing with trouble on his mind/ To leave his native country and his darling girl behind / Oh, his darling girl behind" (Jack - A -Roe) extends the line "Oh, I'm sailin' away my own true love / I'm sailin' away in the morning / Is there something I can send you from across the sea / From the place that I'll be landing?" (Boots Of Spanish Leather).

He writes "Feel bad this morning, ain't got no home" (World Gone Wrong), which extends the line "Well, I woke up in the morning / There's frogs inside my socks" (On The Road Again) and the line "I ain't got no home, I'm just a-roamin' 'round" (I Ain't Got No Home).

"Pack up my suitcase, give me my hat, / No use to ask me, baby, 'cause I'll never be back" (World Gone Wrong) extends the line "Well, it's march me away to the station / With my suitcase in my hand" (Little Maggie).

He writes "Lord, I'm broke, I'm hungry, ragged and dirty too, / Broke and hungry, ragged and dirty too. / If I clean up, sweet momma, can I stay all night with you?" (Ragged & Dirty), which extends the line "'Twas in another lifetime, one of toil and blood / When blackness was a virtue and the road was full of mud / I came in from the wilderness, a creature void of form / "Come in," she said, "I'll give you shelter from the storm"" (Shelter From The Storm).

He writes " 'Cause I'm leaving in the morning, if I have to ride the blinds, / Leaving in the morning, if I have to ride the blinds. / Well, I been mistreated and I swear I don't mind dyin' " (Ragged & Dirty), which probably extends the line "I'm a-leavin' tomorrow, but I could leave today / Somewhere down the road someday / The very last thing that I'd want to do / Is to say I've been hittin' some hard travelin' too" (Song To Woody).

"You don't want me, give my money back / Hey, hey, babe, I got blood in my eyes for you" (Blood In My Eyes) extends the line "Mama wipe the blood off of my face / I can't see through it anymore / I need someone to talk to, and a new hiding place / I feel like I'm looking at heaven's door" (Knocking on Heaven's Door, Live 1975 version).

—*Time Out Of Mind (1997)*

"I see lovers in the meadow / I see silhouettes in the window" (Love Sick) extends the line "Black crows in the meadow / Sleeping across a broad highway" (Black Crow Blues).

"She threw me outside, / I stood in the dirt where ev'ryone walked. / And after finding I'd / Forgotten my shirt, / I went back and knocked." (One of Us Must Know, Sooner Or Later) is connected to "Gonna walk down that dirt road" (Dirt Road Blues).

"Gonna walk down that dirt road, until my eyes begin to bleed / 'Til there's nothing left to see 'Til the chains have been shattered and I been freed (Dirt Road Blues) extends the line "You don't want me, give my money back / Hey, hey, babe, I got blood in my eyes for you" (Blood In My Eyes).

"But I been looking at my shadow, I been watching the clouds up above / looking at my shadow, watching the clouds up above / Rolling through the rain and hail Looking for the sunny side of love" (Dirt Road Blues) extends several lines, for instance "And the clouds are weeping" (Love Sick).

"I been ridin a midnight train / Got ice water in my veins / I would be crazy if I took you back / It would go up against every rule" (Standin' On The Doorway) extends the line "Well, I ride on a mailtrain, baby / Can't buy a thrill / Well, I've been up all night, baby / Leanin' on the windowsill / Well, if I die / On top of the hill / And if I don't make it / You know my baby will" (It Takes A Lot To Laugh, It Takes A Train To Cry).

He writes "I can hear the church bells ringin' in the yard / I wonder who they're ringin' for? / I know I can't win / But my heart just won't give in" (Standin' On The Doorway), which extends the line he sang "Did you ever hear them church bells toll / Means another poor boy is dead and gone" (See That My Grave Is Kept Clean), which lead us to think that Dylan is thinking of the young lover who is dead —because he cannot succeed in love— and gone down the road for the love sake. That line extends as well "Ring them bells, for the time that flies / For the child that cries / When innocence dies" (Ring Them Bells).

He writes "You left me standing out in the cold" (Milllion Miles), which extends the line "You left me standing in the doorway cryin'" (Standin' On The Doorway).

"There's a rumbling in the skies / I've been wading through the high muddy water" (Trying To Get To Heaven) extends the line "Means farewell, Angelina, the sky is trembling and I must leave " (Farewell Angelina). Dylan writes "I've been wading through the high muddy water / With the heat rising in my eyes / I've been walking through the middle of nowhere / Trying to get to heaven before they close the door" (Trying To Get To Heaven), which extends the line "Twas in another lifetime, one of toil and blood / When blackness was a virtue the road was full of mud / I came in from the wilderness, a creature void of form / Come in, she said, I'll give you shelter from the storm" (Shelter From The Storm).

He writes "I'm going down the river / Down to New Orleans / They tell me everything is gonna be all right / But I don't know what "all right" even means" (Trying To Get To Heaven), which extends the line "I'm goin' down to New Orleans, baby, behind the rising sun / Goin' down to New Orleans, baby, behind the rising sun / Lord, I've just found out, my trouble has just begun" (Going Down To New Orleans).

"My eyes feel / Like they're fallin' off my face / Sweat fallin' down / I'm starin' at the floor" (Til I Fell In Love With You) extends the line "It's gettin' dark, too dark for me to see / Mama, put my guns in the ground / That long black cloud is comin' down" (Knockin' On Heavens Door) and "And even if the flesh falls off of my face / I know someone will be there to care" (Standing In The Doorway).

He writes "She wrote me a letter and she wrote it so kind / She put down in writin' what was in her mind / I just don't see why I should even care / It's not dark yet, but it's getting there" (Not Dark Yet), which extends the line "I got a letter on a lonesome day / It was from her ship a-sailin' / Saying I don't know when I'll be comin' back again / It depends on how I'm a-feelin'" (Boots Of Spanish Leather).

He writes "I was born here and I'll die here, against my will / I know it looks like I'm movin' but I'm standin' still" (Not Dark Yet), which extends the line "I was born in Dixie in a boomer shed / Just a little shanty by the railroad track / Freight train was it taught me how to cry / The holler of the driver was my lullaby / I got the freight train blues / Oh Lord mama, I got them in the bottom of my rambling shoes / And when the whistle blows I gotta go baby, don't you know / Well, it looks like I'm never gonna lose the freight train blues" (Freight Train Blues).

He writes "Well, the road is rocky and the hillside's mud / Up over my head nothing but clouds of blood" (Cold Irons Bound), which extends among others, the following lines: "I've stumbled on the side of twelve misty mountains" (A Hard Rain's A Gonna Fall); "Gonna walk down that dirt road, until my eyes begin to bleed" (Dirt Road Blues); "Hey, hey, babe, I got blood in my eyes for you" (Blood In My Eyes); "Mama wipe the blood off of my face / I can't see through it anymore" (Knocking on Heaven's Door, Live 1975 version); "The gravel road is bumpy / It's a hard road to ride / But there's a clearer road a-waitin' / With the cinders on the side" (Paths Of Victory), and "When blackness was a virtue and the road was full of mud" (Shelter From The Storm.)

He writes "The storms are raging on the rollin' sea / And on the highway of regret / The winds of change are blowing wild and free / You ain't seen nothing like me yet" (Make you feel my love), which extends the line "So take heed, take heed of the western wind / Take heed of the stormy weather" (Boots of Spanish Leather) and "May your hands always be busy / May your feet always be swift / May you have a strong foundation / When the winds of changes shift" (Forever Young).

—Love And Theft (2001)

He writes "Well, the rain beating down on my windowpane / I got love for you and it's all in vain" (Tweedle Dee & Tweedle Dum), which extends the line "Sign on the window says "Lonely" / Looks like a-nothing but rain ..." (Sign On The Window).

He writes "City's just a jungle; / trapped in the heart of it, tryin' to get away / I was raised in the country, I been workin' in the town / I been in trouble ever since I set my suitcase down" (Mississippi), which extends the line "Well, I'm walkin' down the highway / With my suitcase in my hand" (Down The Highway), "Right now I'm havin' trouble / Please don't take away my highway shoes" (Down The Highway), and "This place ain't doing me any good / I'm in the wrong town, I should be in Hollywood" (Things Have Changed). He writes "Sky full of fire, pain pourin' down / Nothing you can sell me, I'll see you around" (Mississippi), which extends the line "Farewell Angelina / The sky is on fire / The sky is embarrassed / The sky is erupting" (Farewell Angelina). He writes "Walkin' through the leaves, falling from the trees / Feelin' like a stranger nobody sees" (Mississippi), which extends the line "I'm ready to go anywhere, I'm ready for to fade / in to my own parade" (Mr. Tambourine Man) and "You're invisible now, you got no secrets to conceal" (Like A Rolling Stone). He writes "I'm gonna look at you 'til my eyes go blind" (Mississippi), which extends the line "Mama, take this badge off of me / I can't use it anymore / It's gettin' dark, too dark for me to see" (Knocking On Heavens Door). He writes "Well my ship's been split to splinters and it's sinkin' fast / I'm drownin' in the poison, got no future, got no past" (Mississippi) which extends the line "Then you better start swimmin' or you'll sink like a stone" (The Times They Are A-Changin') and the line "Then I'll stand on the ocean until I start sinkin'" (A Hard Rain's A-Gonna Fall). He writes "But my heart is not weary, it's light and it's free" (Mississippi), which extends the line "lay down your weary tune, lay down" (Lay Down Your Weary Tune).

He writes "I got a house on a hill, I got hogs out lying in the mud / I Got a long haired woman, she got royal Indian blood" (Summer Days), which extends the line "I've stumbled on the side of twelve misty mountains" (A Hard Rain's A Gonna Fall) and "When blackness was a virtue and the road was full of mud" (Shelter From The Storm).

He writes "Where do you come from? Where do you go?" (Summer Days), which extends the line "Oh, where have you been, my blue-eyed son?" and "Oh, what'll you do now, my blue-eyed son?" (A Hard Rain's A Gonna Fall).

He writes, "Well, I'm leaving in the morning as soon as the dark clouds lift / Yes, I'm leaving in the morning just as soon as the dark clouds lift / Gonna break in the roof, set fire to the place as a parting gift" (Summer Days), which extends the line "I'm a-leavin' tomorrow, but I could leave today" (Song To Woody) and the line "oh, they're burning down the house I was brung up in, and they're shouting come on out and take your bride" (Rocky Mountain Belle, Ramblin' Jack Elliot).

He writes "Well, the road's washed out—weather not fit for man or beast" (Lonesome Day Blues), which extends among others this line: "I came in from the wilderness, a creature void of form" (Shelter From The Storm).

He writes "Down over the window / Comes the dazzling sunlit rays / Through the back alleys—through the blinds / Another one of them endless days" (Floater, Too Much To Ask) which extends the line "Standing on your window, honey / Yes, I've been here before" (Temporary Like Achilles).

He writes "Don't reach out for me," she said / "Can't you see I'm drownin' too?" / It's rough out there / High water everywhere (High Water, For Charley Patton), which extends the line "And admit that the waters / Around you have grown" (The Times They Are A-Changin'); and he writes "Thunder rolling over Clarksdale, everything is looking blue" (High Water, For Charley Patton), which extends the line "I'm a-goin' back out 'fore the rain starts a-fallin' / And it's a hard, it's a hard, it's a hard, it's a hard / It's a hard rain's a-gonna fall" (A Hard Rain's A-Gonna Fall), which extends the line

57

"Looks like we'll be blessed with a little more rain, / Four feet high and risin'" (Five Feet High And Rising, Johnny Cash).

"Man comes to the door—I say, "For whom are you looking?" / He says, "Your wife," I say, "She's busy in the kitchen cookin'" / Poor boy—where you been? / I already tol' you—won't tell you again /Poor boy—dressed in black / Police at your back" (Poor Boy) extends the line "You caused me to leave old Kingsport Town / With a high sheriff on my trail / High sheriff on my trail, boys / High sheriff on my trail / All because I'm falling for / A curly-headed dark-eyed girl (Kingsport Town).

—*Modern Times (2006)*

"Thunder on the mountain, fires on the moon / There's a ruckus in the alley and the sun will be here soon / Thunder on the mountain rolling to the ground / Gonna get up in the morning walk the hard road down / Gonna raise me an army" (Thunder On The Mountain), that extends the line "I saw that silver linin' / That was hangin' in the sky / Trails of troubles / Roads of battles" (Paths Of Victory).

"Woke up this mornin', I must have bet my money wrong (Rollin' and Tumblin') extends the line "I woke in the mornin', wand'rin' / Wasted and worn out" (Black Crow Blues) and the line "Well, I woke up in the morning / There's frogs inside my socks" (On The Road Again).

"The midnight rain follows the train / We all wear the same thorny crown" (When The Deal Goes Down) is connected to "And it's a hard, and it's a hard, it's a hard, and it's a hard / And it's a hard rain's a-gonna fall" (A Hard Rain's A-Gonna Fall), to the line "Well, I ride on a mailtrain, baby / Can't buy a thrill / Well, I've been up all night, baby / Leanin' on the windowsill" (It Takes A Lot To Laugh, It Takes A Train To Cry), and to the line "She walked up to me so gracefully and took my crown of thorns / "Come in," she said, "I'll give you shelter from the storm"" (Shelter From The Storm).

He writes "Albert's in the graveyard, Frankie's raising hell" (Nettie Moore), which extends the line "Frankie pulled out a pistol. / Pulled out a forty-four. / Gun went off a rootie-toot-toot / And Albert fell on the floor" (Frankie & Albert). In the same song, Dylan writes "I loved you then and ever shall / But there's no one here that's left to tell / The world has gone black before my eyes" (Nettie Moore), which extends the line "Where black is the color, where none is the number" (A Hard Rain's A Gonna Fall).

"If it keep on rainin' the levee gonna break / I tried to get you to love me, but I won't repeat that mistake" (The Levee's Gonna Break) extends the line "Where the pellets of poison are flooding their waters" (A Hard Rain's A Gonna Fall).

—*Together Through Life (2009)*

He writes "Well my ship is in the harbor / And the sails are spread" (Beyond Here Lies Nothin'), which extends the line "Oh, I'm sailin' away my own true love / I'm sailin' away in the morning" (Boots Of Spanish Leather).

"Listen to me, pretty baby / Lay your hand upon my head / Beyond here lies nothin' / Nothing done and nothing said" (Beyond Here Lies Nothin') extends the line "Still I wish there was somethin' you would do or say / To try and make me change my mind and stay / We never did too much talkin' anyway" (Don't Think Twice, It's All Right).

He writes "I'll sleep by your door, lay my life on the line" (Jolene), which extends the line "Your lover who just walked out the door, / has taken all his blankets from your floor" (It's All Over Now, Baby Blue) and the line "Temptation's page flies out the door" (It's Alright, Ma, I'm Only Bleeding).

"How long can I stay in this nowhere café / 'fore night turns into day / I wonder why I'm so frightened of dawn / All I have and all I know / Is this dream of you / Which keeps me living on" (This Dream Of You) extends the line "When your rooster crows at the break of dawn / Look out your window and I'll be gone / You're the reason I'm trav'lin' on" (Don't Think Twice, It's All Right) and the line "Though I know that evenin's empire has returned into sand / Vanished from my hand / Left me blindly here to stand but still not sleeping / My weariness amazes me, I'm branded on my feet / I have no one to meet / And the ancient empty street's too dead for dreaming / Hey! Mr. Tambourine Man, play a song for me / In the jingle jangle morning I'll come followin' you" (Mr. Tambourine Man.)

"Come back here we can have some real fun / Well it's early in the evening and everything is still / One more time, I'm walking up on heartbreak hill" (Shake Shake Mama) extends the line "I'm

60

lookin' good to see you, yeah, and we can have some fun / One more weekend, one more weekend with you" (One More Weekend).

"And I just can't wait / Wait for us to become friends" (I Feel A Change Comin' On) extends the line "All I really want to do / Is, baby, be friends with you" (All I Really Want To Do).

—*Tempest (2012)*

In "Duquesne Whistle" Dylan speaks again about love, "You're the only thing alive that keeps me going", and he underlines that love could be dangerous, "You're like a time bomb in my heart", and that's what this tune is all about: "Can't you hear that Duquesne whistle blowing? / Blowing like the sky's gonna blow apart". It's not the first time that he speaks of sky in these terms; for instance, "Farewell, Angelina" goes "The sky is on fire / the sky is trembling / the sky is folding / the sky is changing colour / the sky is erupting, I must go where it's quiet" and "This sky, too, is folding under you / And it's all over now, Baby Blue" (It's All Over Now, Baby Blue).

He writes "That Duquesne train gon' rock me night and day" (Duquesne Whistle) which extends the line "Well, I ride on a mailtrain, baby / Can't buy a thrill / Well, I've been up all night, baby / Leanin' on the windowsill" (It Takes A Lot To Laugh, It Takes A Train To Cry).

He writes "You smiling through the fence at me / Just like you've always smiled before" (Duquesne Whistle), which extends the line "Of course, you're gonna think this song is a riff / I know you're gonna think this song is a cliff / Unless you've been inside a tunnel /

And fell down 69, 70 feet over a barbed-wire fence / All night!" (Sitting On A Barbed Wire Fence).

        Dylan said: "All these songs are connected. Don't be fooled. I just opened up a different door in a different kind of way. It's just different, saying the same thing." (Speech on MusiCares Person of the Year, 2015). We have pointed out some of the links and connexions that are there throughout Dylan's poetry. We could have missed some, and, for sure, we haven't pointed out all of them. Pointing out all of them might be impossible to do. Any attentive reader of Dylan's poetry might find other connexions. What's important at this point is to keep in mind that Dylan is saying the same thing in a different way. What is that thing he's talking about?

3. The context of a significant part of Dylan's poetry: A contemporary love-song book.

After having established some connexions and links throughout Dylan's poetry, it's time to put two questions: a) Why are those verses connected? We could replay as follows: those verses are all connected, first of all, because the vast majority of them are dealing with the same topic, that is love; and, secondly, because there are some similarities in the expressions Dylan uses to refer to the same topic (love), however there are always new ways of referring to the same reality. I will come back to this point later. b) Why are those connections and links that important in Dylan's poetry? We could replay as follows: those connexions and links throughout Dylan's poetry are definitely important, because they give us the context in which we can read a significant part of Dylan's poetry in a way that makes sense, and that context is a contemporary love-song book. c) Why is that the right context to read Dylan's poetry? Because Dylan is always talking about the same thing —a great love-story— and he refers to it with expressions that are similar and different at the same time.

The road Bob Dylan is talking about is love and he has created his own way to talk about it throughout his poetry. He has created his own expressions and ways of referring to love. Every single love-song in this contemporary love-song book works as a love-song poem, but in order to understand what Dylan is talking about in any love-song poem, the reader needs to put every single love-song in the right context. The right context is a contemporary love-song book. If the reader doesn't read Dylan in this wide context, he will probably not grasp what Dylan is referring to, as we saw in the introduction.

It takes a first reading throughout Dylan's poetry to get the connexions based on which he has built up his contemporary love-song book and to be familiar with the expressions with which Dylan writes about love. That's what we have done in the first part of this research. Now, once we are in the right context, we can start a second reading throughout Dylan's poetry in which we can understand some expressions that in the first one were totally locked. That's what we are going to do in this second part of this research.

Going back to the question 'Why are Dylan's verses interconnected throughout his albums?', we can answer that probably because he's telling us always about the same old story, but any time he does it in a different way. Let us put it this way: from a poetic point of view, Dylan's always dealing with the same love-story, but he comes up constantly with new ways of writing about it, based on what he wrote earlier. From that perspective, what Dylan said makes sense, "I thought I was just extending the line. Maybe a little bit unruly, but I was just elaborating on situations." Indeed, he was just elaborating on love situations and he has created his own way to tell one great love-story. What story is that? We will try to explain it in the pages that follow.

a) The protagonist of that love-story is an outlaw.

Dylan has sung many times old tunes about outlaws, for instance, "They took me off the Georgia Main / Locked me to a ball and chain / I heard that lonesome whistle blow" (Lonesome Whistle

Blues), and here he is writing and singing about outlaws who fall in love and while on the run: "Don't you remember me babe / I remember you quite well / You caused me to leave old Kingsport Town / With a high sheriff on my trail / High sheriff on my trail, boys / High sheriff on my trail / All because I'm falling for / A curly-headed dark-eyed girl (Kingsport Town), "Well they took me down town and they dressed me in black, / They put me on a train and they sent me back / They crammed me back into the county jail / Forty-one years to wear the ball and the stripes" (In Search Of Little Sadie), and "They ask me how I feel / They'd like to drive me from this town / They don't want me around / And I walk out on my own / A thousand miles from home" (Slow Train Coming).

You can see outlaws throughout Dylan's albums, and many times the outlaw he is talking about is a young boy: "Man comes to the door—I say, "For whom are you looking?" / He says, "Your wife," I say, "She's busy in the kitchen cookin'" / Poor boy—where you been? / I already tol' you—won't tell you again /Poor boy—dressed in black / Police at your back" (Poor Boy).

b) The protagonist of the story is always looking for love, which is a source of motivation and positive energy.

It's love that makes the protagonist of the story to be alive: "You're the only thing alive that keeps me going" (Duquesne Whistle). The protagonist of the story is always somewhere down the road looking for love: "Highway 51 runs right by my baby's door / If I don't get the girl I'm loving / Won't go down to Highway 51 no more" (Highway 51 Blues), which is connected to that old tune Dylan recorded "Well he rode up to Miss Mousey's door / gave three loud raps and a very big roar, Uh-huh." (Froggie Went A-Courtin') and "Took Miss Mousey on his knee / said, "Miss Mousey, will you marry me?" Uh-huh" (Froggie Went A-Courtin'), which is connected to "Would you marry me, Pretty Peggy-O / Would you marry me, your cities I will free" (Pretty Peggy-O), and to "I'm just goin' down the road t' see Bessie / Oh, see her soon / Goin' down the road t' see Bessie Smith / When I get there I wonder what she''l do" (Bessie Smith).

The protagonist of Dylan's great love-story is always in the mood to look for love: "And sometimes I'm in the mood, I wanna hit that highway road / but then again, but then again, I said oh, I said oh, I said / oh, babe, I'm in a mood for you" (I'm In A Mood For You), "Your cracked country lips / I still wish to kiss / As to be under the strength of your skin" (Ramona), "Oh, but if I had the stars from the darkest night / And the diamonds from the deepest ocean / I'd forsake them all for your sweet kiss / For that's all I'm wishin' to be ownin.'" (Boots of Spanish Leather), and "Like a needle in a haystack, I'm gonna find you yet, / You're the sweetest gone mama that this boy's ever gonna get" (One More Weekend).

The protagonist of the story usually is looking forward to finding what he wishes: "But the good road is a-waiting / And boys it ain't far off" (Paths of Victory) and "The way is long but the end is near" (Romance In Durango). In this context of desiring, the road is on fire: "This wheel's on fire / Rolling down the road / Best notify my next of kin / This wheel shall explode!" (This Wheel's On Fire) and "Crimson flames tied through my ears / Rollin' high and mighty traps / Pounced with fire on flaming roads / Using ideas as my maps / "We'll meet on edges, soon," said I" (My Back pages).

Speaking of maps, the lover eventually needs one to make it for the place where love is, and sometimes a key is needed as well, that's probably why Dylan wrote and sang "You're the one I've been looking for, / You're the one that's got the key" (Tight Connexion To My Heart, Has Anybody Seen My Love) and, of course, "You gimme a map and a key to your door" (Sara).

The protagonist calls the lover to make it happen: "Won't you come see me, Queen Jane?" (Queen Jane Approximately), "Well, I wanna be your lover, baby / I don't wanna be your boss" (It Takes A Lot To Laugh, It Takes A Train To Cry), "Won't you come with me, baby? / I'll take you where you wanna go / And if it don't work out / You'll be the first to know / I'm pledging my time to you / Hopin' you'll come through, too" (Pledging My Time), "Slippin' and slidin' like a weasel on the run / I'm lookin' good to see you, yeah, and we can have some fun" (One More Weekend), and "We'll both just sit there and stare / Me with my belt / Wrapped around my head / And you just sittin' there / In your brand new leopard-skin pill-box hat" (Leopard-Skil Pill Box Hat), which is connected to "Standin' on the highway, you flag me down / Said, take me Daddy, to the nearest town / You got a rag wrapped around your head / Wearing a long dress fire engine red" (Had A Dream About You, Baby).

Once in a while, the protagonist of the story succeeds: "Oh you five and ten cent women / With nothin' in your heads / I got a real gal I'm lovin' / And Lord I'll love her till I'm dead / Go away from my door and my window too / Right now" (Bob Dylan's Blues), "Can't you hear that rooster crowin'? / So happy just to see you smile / Underneath the sky of blue / On this new morning with you" (New Morning). For once on the road the door is easy to open, that's probably why Dylan wrote: "Sara, Sara, / It's all so clear, I could never forget, / Sara, Sara, / Lovin' you is the one thing I'll never regret" (Sara). But usually it's difficult to succeed in love. Even if the protagonist fails, he has to move forward and try again: "Was in the summer, / One early fall / Was in the spring, / One summer's day. / Now she's gone / I'm sittin' on top of the world. / Went to the station, / Down in the yard, / Gonna get me a freight train (Sittin' On Top Of The World), which is connected to "I got the freight train blues / Oh Lord mama, I got them in the bottom of my rambling shoes / And when the whistle blows I gotta go baby, don't you know / Well, it looks like I'm never gonna lose the freight train blues" (Freight Train Blues).

c) However, the protagonist of the story realizes that love is difficult to hold on to.

Dylan has sung many times tunes on the trouble the protagonist of his story faces: "I'm goin' down to New Orleans, baby, behind the rising sun / Goin' down to New Orleans, baby, behind the rising sun / Lord, I've just found out, my trouble has just begun" (Going Down To New Orleans), which is connected to "I'm going down the river / Down to New Orleans / They tell me everything is gonna be all right / But I don't know what "all right" even means" (Trying To Get To Heaven), to "Yes, I'm walkin' down the highway / With my suitcase in my hand / Lord, I really miss my baby / She's in some far-off land" (Down The Highway), to "Well, it's march me away to the station / With my suitcase in my hand, / Yes, march me away to the station, / I'm off to some far-distant land (Little Maggie), to "Right now I'm havin' trouble / Please don't take away my highway shoes" (Down The Highway), to "Well, I'm a-walkin' down the road / With my head in my hand / I'm lookin' for a woman / Needs a worried man" (Honey, Just Allow Me One More Chance), and to "Well, lookin' for a woman / That ain't got no man / Is just lookin' for a needle / That is lost in the sand" (Honey, Just Allow Me One More Chance). "Paths Of Victory" is about that: "I walked down by the river / I turned my head up high / I saw that silver linin' / That was hangin' in the sky / Trails of troubles / Roads of battles" (Paths Of Victory). The protagonist has to work hard to succeed in finding love to the extent that he needs an army: "Thunder on the mountain, fires on the moon / There's a ruckus in the alley and the sun will be here soon / Thunder on the mountain rolling to the ground / Gonna get up in the morning walk the hard road down / Gonna raise me an army" (Thunder On The Mountain).

At a certain point, the protagonist of the story feels like it's all about trouble: "Since the beginning of the universe man's been cursed by trouble / Trouble / Trouble, trouble, trouble / Nothin' but trouble" (Trouble). Indeed, he's been always in trouble: "City's just a jungle; / trapped in the heart of it, tryin' to get away / I was raised in the country, I been workin' in the town / I been in trouble ever since I set my suitcase down" (Mississippi).

But even knowing that love is difficult to reach and to hold on to, the lover tries once and again: "Well, I ride on a mailtrain, baby / Can't buy a thrill / Well, I've been up all night, baby / Leanin' on the windowsill / Well, if I die / On top of the hill / And if I don't make it / You know my baby will" (It Takes A Lot To Laugh, It Takes A Train To Cry), "Don't let me down" (Obviously Five Believers), "Oh, sister, when I come to knock on your door / Don't turn away, you'll create sorrow" (Oh, Sister).

Let us put it this way: love is a rough experience you have to try out: "There's a new day at dawn and I've finally arrived / If I'm there in the morning, baby, you'll know I've survived" (Where Are You Tonight? Journey Through Dark Heat); and that experience you have to try out covers all your life from the beginning to the end: "I don't care how rough the road is, show me where it starts" (What Can I Do For You), which is connected to "I was born very far from where I was supposed to be, so I'm on my way home" (No Direction Home) and to "Come baby, find me, come baby, remind me of where I once begun" (Emotionally Yours).

The protagonist experiences that love is difficult to find, and if he finds it, it's too difficult to hold on to, because, on one hand, it's slippery: "Never could learn to hold you, love / And call you mine" (Tight Connexion To My Heart, Has Anybody Seen My Love), which is related to "I married Isis on the fifth day of May / But I could not hold on to her very long" (Isis); and, on the other hand, because it's always about to come to an end: "You're like a time bomb in my heart" (Duquesne Whistle); then, loves becomes tragedy.

Love it's difficult to find, and at the beginning of his contemporary love-song book Dylan cares about it: "I can't understand / She let go of my hand / An' left me here facing the wall" (I Don't Believe You, She Acts Like We Never Have Met), "I courted her proudly but now she is gone / Gone as the season she's taken" (Ballad in Plain D); but at a certain point he doesn't care about it: "I can keep both feet on the ground / I can follow the path, I can read the signs / I can handle whatever I stumble upon / I don't even notice she's gone" (Most Of The Time), which is related to "I don't care what you do, I don't care what you say / I don't care where you go or how long you stay" (Someday Baby), which extends the line "Now she's gone, / An' I don't worry / Lord, I'm sittin' on top of the world" (Sittin' On Top Of The World).

That failed search for love is the context in which the protagonist of Dylan's contemporary love-song book is trapped: "I was born here and I'll die here, against my will / I know it looks like I'm movin' but I'm standin' still" (Not Dark Yet).

Probably because love is difficult to find and to hold on to, Dylan writes "May you build a ladder to the stars / And climb on every rung" (Forever Young).

d) Actually, the protagonist of the story finds out that love hurts, because you cannot hold on to it.

The protagonist of the story doesn't want to hurt anybody, but he does: "An' I told you, as you clawed out my eyes / That I never really meant to do you any harm" (One Of Us Must Know, Sooner Or Later) and "Oh ev'ry girl that ever I've touched / I did not do it harmfully / And ev'ry girl that ever I've hurt / I did not do it knowin'ly" (Restless Farewell). Love hurts because it's difficult to keep and it gives way to separation, that always hurts: "One more night, the moon is shinin' bright / And the wind blows high above the tree / Oh, I miss that woman so" (One More Night).

Dylan writes "He was just a blue-eyed Boston boy, / (...) There's no one to write to the blue-eyed girl / the words that her lover had said. / Momma, you know, awaits the news, / And she'll only know he's dead" (Two Soldiers), which is related to "Oh, where have you been, my blue-eyed son? / Oh, where have you been, my darling young one?" (A Hard Rain's A Gonna Fall), which leads us to think that probably the blue-eyed son Dylan talks about in A Hard Rain's A Gonna Fall has been dealing with difficulties in love. He has been trying hard, but it didn't work, which is probably why he writes: "I've stumbled on the side of twelve misty mountains / I've walked and I've crawled on six crooked highways / I've stepped in the middle of seven sad forests / I've been out in front of a dozen dead oceans / I've been ten thousand miles in the mouth of a graveyard" (A Hard Rain's A Gonna Fall). In this context, "stumbling on", "walking", and "stepping in" are actions that take place on the road, on that fight for love that is difficult to find. Love hurts, to the point that love breaks you: "Streets are filled with broken hearts" (Everything Is Broken), "Broken bodies, broken bones" (Everything Is Broken). I will come back to difficulties in love and the way Dylan expresses them throughout his contemporary love-song book.

e) Love doesn't work because of the way the lover is.

ea) The lover is hard.

"Señor, señor, you know their heart is as hard as leather" (Senor, Tales Of Yankee Power) extends the line "And yes, there's something you can send back to me / Spanish boots of Spanish leather" (Boots of Spanish Leather), which is connected to "Pull off, pull off them high-heeled shoes / All made of Spanish leather" (Black Jack Davey). Those connexions go back to "Boots of Spanish Leather" that is a song about failed love. The fact that the lover is hard is expressed in other verses that are linked: "When she's near me she's so hard to recognize" (True Love Tends To Forget) and "so easy to look at, so hard to define" (Sara).

eb) The lover mistreats the protagonist of the story.

"When I come knocking don't throw me no bone / I'm an old boll weevil looking for a home" (Silvio), "'Cause I'm leaving in the morning, if I have to ride the blinds, / Leaving in the morning, if I have to ride the blinds. / Well, I been mistreated and I swear I don't mind dyin' " (Ragged & Dirty), and "They say the darkest hour is right before the dawn / Little rooster crowin', there must be something on his mind / Well, I feel just like that rooster / Honey, ya treat me so unkind" (Meet Me in the Morning).

ec) The lover is silent, so the protagonist of the story doesn't know what's going on.

"My love she speaks like silence / my love she speaks softly" (Love Minus Zero/No Limit) is related to "Not a word was spoke between us, there was little risk involved / Everything up to that point had been left unresolved" (Shelter From The Storm). There are not words, so there's no solution for the lovers to stick together even if they would like to: "Still I wish there was somethin' you would do or say / To try and make me change my mind and stay / We never did too much talkin' anyway" (Don't Think Twice It's All Right) and "I'd forever talk to you / But soon my words / They would turn into a meaningless ring / For deep in my heart / I know there is no help I can bring / Everything passes / Everything changes" (Ramona).

Lack of communication sometimes hurts: "Alberta what's on your mind / Alberta what's on your mind / You keep me worried and bothered / All of the time / Alberta what's on your mind / Alberta don't you treat me unkind / Alberta don't you treat me unkind / Oh my heart is so sad / Cause I want you so bad / Alberta don't you treat me unkind" (Alberta #1) and "Not a word of goodbye, not even a note / She gone with the man / In the long black coat" (Man In The Long Black Coat).

Sometimes the lover tries to communicate: "Just a minute before you leave, girl / Just a minute before you touch the door / What is it that you're trying to achieve, girl? / Do you think we can talk about it some more? / You know the streets are filled with vipers / Who've lost all ray of hope" (Don't Fall Appear On Me Tonight) and "Listen to me, pretty baby / Lay your hand upon my head / Beyond here lies nothin' / Nothing done and nothing said" (Beyond Here Lies Nothin').

ed) The lover blinds the protagonist of the story and acts against him.

Indeed: "Sweet Goddess / Born of a blinding light and a changing wind, / Now, don't be modest, / you know who you are and where you've been" (Tough Mama) is linked to "I'm gonna look at you 'til my eyes go blind" (Mississippi) and also to "Gonna walk down that dirt road, until my eyes begin to bleed / 'Til there's nothing left to see 'Til the chains have been shattered and I been freed (Dirt Road Blues), which extends the line "Mama wipe the blood off of my face / I can't see through it anymore / I need someone to talk to, and a new hiding place / I feel like I'm looking at

74

heaven's door" (Knocking on Heaven's Door, Live 1975 version) and the line "You don't want me, give my money back / Hey, hey, babe, I got blood in my eyes for you" (Blood In My Eyes). Everything turns black in the presence of the lover: "I loved you then and ever shall / But there's no one here that's left to tell / The world has gone black before my eyes" (Nettie Moore) probably extends the line "Where black is the color, where none is the number" (A Hard Rain's A Gonna Fall).

The lover transmits a blinding light and a wind that changes direction, and that makes it more difficult to reach it. In the context of love, when the lover asks the lover where you've been, it means so to speak, how did it go trying love out there going down the road? And the answer is it was horrible, because the lover always blinds you and when you are trying to get there the wind blows strong and changes. I guess that's the framework to make some sense of songs like A Hard Rain's A Gonna Fall. The question now is "what did you hear, my blue-eyed son", because during the encounter with the lover the protagonist of the story doesn't see, the protagonist goes blind, for the presence of the lover is magnificent, strong, terrible, like thunder, like a big wave, and it's difficult to reach: "And what did you hear, my blue-eyed son? / And what did you hear, my darling young one? / I heard the sound of a thunder, it roared out a warnin' / Heard the roar of a wave that could drown the whole world / Heard one hundred drummers whose hands were a-blazin' / Heard ten thousand whisperin' and nobody listenin' / Heard one person starve, I heard many people laughin' / Heard the song of a poet who died in the gutter / Heard the sound of a clown who cried in the alley / And it's a hard, and it's a hard, it's a hard, it's a hard / And it's a hard rain's a-gonna fall" (A Hard Rain's A-Gonna Fall). It's in this context that lines like the following make sense: "For all eternity I think I will remember / That icy wind that's howling in your eye" (When The Night Comes Falling From The Sky) make sense.

There's no doubt, the protagonist of the story (the outlaw) goes blind before the lover and suffers a lot: "Once there was a man who had no eyes / Every lady in the land told him lies / He stood beneath the silver sky and his heart began to bleed" (Unbelievable) is linked to "My eyes feel / Like they're fallin' off my face / Sweat fallin' down / I'm starin' at the floor" (Til I Fell In Love With You), which extends the line "It's gettin' dark, too dark for me to see / Mama, put my guns in the ground / That long black cloud is comin' down" (Knockin' On Heavens Door) and the line "And even if the flesh falls off of my face / I know someone will be there to care" (Standing In The Doorway).

It's precisely because the protagonist (the outlaw) goes blind before the lover that he needs to say "Mama, take this badge off of me / I can't use it anymore / It's gettin' dark, too dark for me to see / I feel like I'm knockin' on heaven's door" (Knocking On Heavens Door). In this context of trying to get to the lover while the outlaw goes blind and fights against the wind, some lines make sense: "The storms are raging on the rollin' sea / And on the highway of regret / The winds of change are blowing wild and free / You ain't seen nothing like me yet" (Make You Feel My Love) probably extends the line "So take heed, take heed of the western wind / Take heed of the stormy weather" (Boots of Spanish Leather).

It's in that context that we can fully understand what Dylan means when he writes "May you have a strong foundation / When the winds of changes shift" (Forever Young).

ee) The lover eventually kills the protagonist of the story.

Things on the road oftentimes don't work out, then the love story becomes tragic, that's why we find in Dylan's poetry images like "Oh, where is little Maggie / Over yonder she stands, / Rifle on her shoulder, / Six-shooter in her hand" (Little Maggie), which extends the line "I saw guns and sharp swords in the hands of young children" (A Hard Rain's A-Gonna Fall).

The tragedy sometimes is mortal: "Frankie pulled out a pistol. / Pulled out a forty-four. / Gun went off a rootie-toot-toot" (Frankie & Albert) is connected to "Albert's in the graveyard, Frankie's raising hell" (Nettie Moore). The fact that the protagonist of the story fails in love is shown in lines like "Somewhere Mama's weeping for her blue-eyed boy / She's holding them little white shoes and that little broken toy" (Man Of Peace), where the little white shoes are probably the ones Dylan refers to in the line "Please don't take away my highway shoes" (Down The Highway), and the reference to failure is done by referring to the death of the outlaw, who is presented here again as a boy. That's why his Mama's crying for him, what clarifies the meaning of the song "A Hard Rain's A Gonna Fall". In this context makes sense that the outlaw hears bells ringing once in a while, that means the closeness of death: "Did you ever hear them church bells toll / Means another poor boy is dead and gone" (See That My Grave Is Kept Clean) is connected to "Ring them bells, for the time that flies / For the child that cries / When innocence dies" (Ring Them Bells). In this context, bell's ringing is connected to the fact that the time of the protagonist of the story is coming to an end and he has to try again even knowing that it's not going to work. That's the way I make sense of lines like "I can hear the church bells ringin' in the yard / I wonder who they're ringin' for? / I know I can't win / But my heart just won't give in" (Standin' On The Doorway).

f) The difficulties to hold on to love and the journey looking for it are expressed by cloudy skies, rain, water, wet and misty places.

Rain is not actually a sign of happiness in Dylan's poetry: "The cryin' rain like a trumpet sang / And asked for no applause" (Lay Down Your Weary Tune). Rather, rain and wet spaces are sign of difficulties to hold on to love, and that's probably why Dylan writes lines like "The wind knocks my window, the room it is wet / The words to say I'm sorry, I haven't found yet" (Ballad in Plain D), "There's a long-distance train rolling through the rain / Tears on the letter I write" (Where Are You Tonight? Journey Through Dark Heat), "Sign on the window says "Lonely" / Looks like a-nothing but rain …" (Sign On The Window), and "Well, the rain beating down on my windowpane / I got love for you and it's all in vain" (Tweedle Dee & Tweedle Dum).

Before the rain, there's cloudy sky, that is a sign that things are not going to work out: "The next day was hangin' day, the sky was overcast and black, / Big Jim lay covered up, killed by a penknife in the back" (Lily, Rosemary and the Jack of Hearts), "They sat together in the park / As the evening sky grew dark" (Simple Twist

Of Fate), "Storm clouds are raging all around my door, / I think to myself I might not take it any more" (The Man In Me), "I stood unwound beneath the skies / And clouds unbound by laws" (Lay Down Your Weary Tune), and "How many times must a man look up / Before he can see the sky?" (Blowing In The Wind). Then, there's rain. It's the lover who sends rain; that's probably why Dylan writes "And Louise holds a handful of rain, temptin' you to defy it" (Visions Of Johanna) and "Oh babe, that fire / Is still smokin' / You were snow, you were rain" (Born In Time). The effort of the lover to hold on to love is also expressed by rain: "If it keep on rainin' the levee gonna break / I tried to get you to love me, but I won't repeat that mistake" (The Levee's Gonna Break) is connected to "Where the pellets of poison are flooding their waters" (A Hard Rain's A Gonna Fall), which refers probably to the rejection of the lover. The protagonist of the story knows that he's going to suffer because he will not be able to hold on to love, but still he's going to be bound to keep on trying, so "Then I'll stand on the ocean until I start sinkin' / But I'll know my song well before I start singin' / And it's a hard, it's a hard, it's a hard, it's a hard / It's a hard rain's a-gonna fall" (A Hard Rain's A-Gonna Fall). Sometimes, the difficulties in love are expressed by high waters: "Well, that high tide's risin' / Mama, don't you let me down / Pack up your suitcase / Mama, don't you make a sound (Crash On The Levee, Down In The Flood), "You know you can't keep her and the water gets deeper / That is leading you onto the brink" (No Time To Think), and "Don't reach out for me," she said / "Can't you see I'm drownin' too?" / It's rough out there / High water everywhere (High Water, For Charley Patton), which is connected to "Looks like we'll be blessed with a little more rain, / Four feet high and risin'" (Five Feet High And Rising, Johnny Cash), tune very well know by Dylan.

It's usually raining in the road the protagonist of the story is walking down, that's why "And he was standin' on the side of the road / Rain fallin' on his shoes" (Tangled Up In Blue); and that's difficult to bear: "Well, the road's washed out—weather not fit for man or beast" (Lonesome Day Blues). However, the protagonist of the story finds some relief when he steps in someone's place and tries love: "I came in from the wilderness, a creature void of form. / "Come in," she said, "I'll give you shelter from the storm" (Shelter From The Storm), that's probably why Dylan writes "When storm clouds gather round you / And heavy rains descend / Just remember that death is not the end (Death Is Not The End).

Those episodes of love happen while he is walking down a dirty and wet road: "'Twas in another lifetime, one of toil and blood / When blackness was a virtue and the road was full of mud" (Shelter From The Storm), "Gon' walk down that dirt road, 'til someone lets me ride" (Dirt Road blues), "Lord, I'm broke, I'm hungry, ragged and dirty too, / Broke and hungry, ragged and dirty too. / If I clean up, sweet momma, can I stay all night with you?" (Ragged & Dirty), and "My clothes are wet, tight on my skin / Not as tight as the corner that I painted myself in / I know that fortune is waitin' to be kind / So give me your hand and say you'll be mine" (Mississippi). After the encounter between lovers and given the impossibility of holding on to love, the lover walks out back to the road again, back to the rain: "Our conversation was short and sweet / It nearly swept me off-a my feet. / And I'm back in the rain, oh / And you are on dry land" (You're A Big Girl Now) and "I'm walking through streets that are dead / Walking, walking with you in my head / My feet are so tired, my brain is so wired / And the clouds are weeping" (Love Sick).

80

After the encounter with the lover, what remains is rain and vague memories, because the lover is back to the road, back to the rain: "The harmonicas play the skeleton keys and the rain / And these visions of Johanna are now all that remain" (Visions Of Johanna).

In this journey, the lover has been walking down the road and undergoing difficulties: "There's a rumbling in the skies / I've been wading through the high muddy water" (Trying To Get To Heaven) and "I've been wading through the high muddy water / With the heat rising in my eyes / I've been walking through the middle of nowhere / Trying to get to heaven before they close the door" (Trying To Get To Heaven), where heaven is the encounter with the lover and that's probably why Dylan writes "That long black cloud is comin' down / I feel like I'm knockin' on heaven's door" (Knocking On Heaven's Door). From the beginning of this contemporary love-song book the road has been difficult to walk down because of the rain and the mud, that's why Dylan writes "The trail is dusty / And my road it might be rough" (Paths Of Victory), which is connected to "Well, the road is rocky and the hillside's mud / Up over my head nothing but clouds of blood" (Cold Irons Bound), which is connected to "I got a house on a hill, I got hogs out lying in the mud / I Got a long haired woman, she got royal Indian blood" (Summer Days), lines which probably extend the line "I've stumbled on the side of twelve misty mountains" (A Hard Rain's A Gonna Fall).

It turns out that the experience the protagonist of the story is undergoing happens to be too everybody else's story: "The midnight rain follows the train / We all wear the same thorny crown" (When The Deal Goes Down) extends the line "She walked up to me

81

so gracefully and took my crown of thorns / "Come in," she said, "I'll give you shelter from the storm"" (Shelter From The Storm).

That's what the road is all about in Dylan's poetry: rain, pain and trying a love that never is going to be held on to; that's probably why the lover says: "Sky full of fire, pain pourin' down / Nothing you can sell me, I'll see you around" (Mississippi) and "I been lookin' at my shadow, I been watching the colors up above / Lookin' at my shadow watching the colors up above / Rolling through the rain and hail, looking for the sunny side of love" (Dirt Road Blues). Going down the road the protagonist of the story meets different lovers: "How did I meet you? I don't know. / A messenger sent me in a tropical storm" (Sara).

Trying to hold on to love ends up being a ladder difficult to climb, for it's wet: "May you build a ladder to the stars and climb on every rung" (Forever Young), which extends the line "I saw a white ladder all covered with water" (A Hard Rain's A Gonna Fall). In that difficult context of trying desperately to hold on to love, which usually doesn't happen, the best option for the lover is to run away: "Oh, what'll you do now, my blue-eyed son? / Oh, what'll you do now, my darling young one? / I'm a-goin' back out 'fore the rain starts a-fallin'" (A Hard Rain's A Gonna Fall).

g) The difficulties of holding on to love and the journey looking for it are expressed by wind as well.

The wind is always a companion of the outlaw in his search for love: "Who's a-gonna kiss your Memphis mouth / When I'm out in the wind" (Kingsport Town) and "The winter wind is blowing strong, in my hands I have no gloves / I wish to myself that I could see the girl I'm thinking of" (Kingsport Town), to the point that wind is one of the elements of the the landscape where a love-scene takes place or it's recalled, so that wind becomes part of the so called *"locus amoenus"*, which Spanish poets at the end of the middle ages and the renaissance usually stablished as background of love-scenes. Dylan proceeds similarly: "Well, if you're travelin' in the north country fair / Where the winds hit heavy on the borderline / Well, if you go when the snowflakes storm/ When the rivers freeze and summer ends (Girl From The North Country), "Twilight on the frozen lake / North wind about to break / On footprints in the snow / Silence down below" (Never Say Goodbye).

h) Looking for love generates confusion.

The protagonist of the story looks desperately for love, but it turns out that it's difficult to hold on to, but still he tries hopelessly over and over again, to the point that he cannot stop looking for it knowing that it's pointless to try because it's not going to work; therefore, he feels trapped in a game that seems to make no sense: "City's just a jungle; more games to play / Trapped in the heart of it, tryin' to get away / I was raised in the country, I been workin' in the town / I been in trouble ever since I set my suitcase down" (Mississippi) extends the line "There must be some way out of here," said the joker to the thief / "There's too much confusion, I can't get no relief / Businessmen, they drink my wine, plowmen dig my earth / None of them along the line know what any of it is worth" (All Along The Watchtower), which is connected to "I'll go along with this charade / Until I can think my way out. / I know it was all a big joke / Whatever it was about (Tight Connexion To My

Heart, Has Anybody Seen My Love), which extends the line "No reason to get excited," the thief, he kindly spoke / "There are many here among us who feel that life is but a joke (All Along The Watchtower).

In this context of always-looked-for and impossible-love and confusion there's no clear limit between success and failure: "My love she speaks softly / She knows there's no success like failure / And that failure's no success at all" (Love Minus Zero, No Limit), and it's not clear what it's all about: "Wishin' my long-lost lover / Will walk to me, talk to me / Tell me what it's all about" (Black Crow Blues).

i) Looking for love generates sadness.

Precisely because love is difficult to hold on to doesn't last too long and when it's gone gives way to sadness, which is expressed in colour blue: "It's all over now baby blue" (It's All Over Now, Baby Blue) is connected to "Tangle up in blue!" (Tangle Up In Blue). On the contrary, when love is still going on or it's still possible, that love is expressed is colour red: "Early one mornin' the sun was shinin', / he was layin' in bed / Wond'rin' if she'd changed at all / If her hair was still red" (Tangle Up In Blue). Besides, the protagonist of the story knows that red colour doesn't last too much, and that after red skies, the storm comes soon: "Farewell Angelina / The sky is on fire / The sky is embarrassed / The sky is erupting" (Farewell Angelina) is related to "Sky full of fire, pain pourin' down / Nothing you can sell me, I'll see you around" (Mississippi).

84

j) The love the protagonist of the story is looking for doesn't exist; it's just a dream.

From the beginning in Dylan's contemporary love-song book, love is just a dream: "But it grieves my heart, love / To see you tryin' to be a part of / A world that just don't exist / It's all just a dream, babe" (Ramona), and the protagonist of the story sees himself as part of that dream: "You're invisible now, you got no secrets to conceal" (Like A Rolling Stone) extends the line "I'm ready to go anywhere, I'm ready for to fade / Into my own parade, cast your dancing spell my way / I promise to go under it" (Mr Tambourine Man).

However, once and again, that dream keeps the protagonist of the story still alive: "How long can I stay in this nowhere café / 'fore night turns into day / I wonder why I'm so frightened of dawn / All I have and all I know / Is this dream of you / Which keeps me living on" (This Dream Of You) extends the line "Though I know that evenin's empire has returned into sand / Vanished from my hand / Left me blindly here to stand but still not sleeping / My weariness amazes me, I'm branded on my feet / I have no one to meet / And the ancient empty street's too dead for dreaming / Hey! Mr. Tambourine Man, play a song for me / In the jingle jangle morning I'll come followin' you" (Mr. Tambourine Man), where "evening's empire" probably refers to the lover who left the protagonist of the story blind and then vanished. However, the protagonist of the story likes his weariness as a result of that failing encounter with the lover, and that's his destiny, that's why "I'm branded on my feet" (Mr. Tambourine Man). In the morning he will keep on moving on listening to a song that keeps him on moving on. I will come back to the tune Dylan is referring to.

What really matters on Dylan's verses is the feeling he shares with us: "I woke in the mornin', wand'rin' / Wasted and worn out / Wishin' my long-lost lover / Will walk to me, talk to me / Tell me what it's all about" (Black Crow Blues). It would be impossible to state whom he's talking about. The best way to make sense of Dylan's poetry is from Dylan's poetry, reading his verses in the right context. It seems that we get the right context when we link and connect his verses properly. In "Black Crow Blues" he's missing love, but at the same time a black crow is not a good sign, that probably means that he's telling us that he understands that there's no place in his poetry for the love he desires. In the Renaissance, poets wrote about impossible love; for instance, Garcilaso de la Vega wrote many of his poems taking inspiration from his impossible love for Isabel Freyre. Throughout history, love led poets onto write about a impossible love, and that's exactly what Dylan is doing: writing and singing about an impossible love, and that's probably why sometimes he — being aware of the impossibility of reaching and holding on to the love he's looking for— tries either a love of friendship, rather than other kind of love: "All I really want to do / Is, baby, be friends with you" (All I Really Want to Do); or a love that he knows that never is going to take place: "You can come to me sometime / Night time, day time / Any time you want" (Black Crow Blues). Dylan writes about the desire of love and the impossibility of finding it: "Black crows in the meadow / Across a broad highway / Though it's funny, honey / I just don't feel much like a / Scarecrow today" (Black Crow Blues). And again, he desires: "Your cracked country lips / I still wish to kiss / As to be under the strength of your skin" (Ramona), but it doesn't work: "But it grieves my heart, love / To see you tryin' to be a part of / A world that just don't exist / It's all just a dream, babe" (Ramona). That love is impossible to reach: "I'd forever talk to you / But soon my words / They would turn into a meaningless ring / For deep in my heart / I know there is no help I can bring / Everything passes / Everything changes." (Ramona).

k) The love-story is about lost love.

Precisely because the love-story is about lost love, Dylan's poetry focuses many times on the moment when everything between the lovers is over:

ka) The moment of separation.

"She packed it all up in a suitcase / Lord, she took it away to Italy, Italy" (Down The Highway). It's been said by critics that in this line Dylan refers to Suze Rotolo. Sometimes, Dylan refers to particular experiences he had in life, of course, but not always. Plus, it would be really difficult to know when he does or when he doesn't. I think that the love-story he's writing throughout his contemporary love-song book transcends Dylanesque particular loving experiences, which are almost impossible to track down in his songs, because Dylan would never tell you about his private life, so it seems that there's no way to link all his verses with particular biographic experiences. Rather, it makes more sense to identify those images of separation as a part of a poetic story. Nobody can link the following line with an specific experience Dylan underwent: "When your rooster crows at the break of dawn / look out your window and I'll be gone; / you're the reason I'm travelling on; /(Don't Think Twice It's

All Right). Who knows who was Dylan thinking of when he came up whit that line! As we know, he was just elaborating on situations, so probably what he was doing was to create the topic of "moment of separation" in the context of a poetic love-story using lines that are all linked and connected. Dylan wrote "You must leave now, take what you need, you think will last / But whatever you wish to keep, you better grab it fast" (It's All Over Now Baby Blue), which is connected to "I'd like to get you to change your mind / But it looks like you won't / Whatever you gonna do / Please do it fast / I'm still trying to get used to / Seeing the real you at last" (Seeing The Real You At Last) and to "The highway is for gamblers, better use your sense / Take what you have gathered from coincidence." (It's All Over Now Baby Blue), and so on: "When you wake up in the mornin', baby, look inside your mirror / You know I won't be next to you, you know I won't be near" (Mama, You Been On My Mind) and "I'm just gonna let you pass, / Yes, and I'll go last. / Then time will tell who fell / And who's been left behind, / When you go your way and I go mine." (Most Likely You Go Your Way I'll Go Mine). The are many lines Dylan wrote on this topic: "Let's call it a day, go our own different ways" (We Better Talk This Over); "I guess I'll be leaving tomorrow" (We Better Talk This Over), etc., we just pointed out some of them.

kb) The reason of separation.

There are some specific reasons of separation throughout Dylan's modern love-song book: "She wants me to be a hero" (Hero Blues), "I'm not the one you want, babe, I'm not the one you need" (It Ain't Me, Babe), and "I just could not be what she wanted me to be" (One More Night).

88

Besides, theres's the danger of harm if love keeps on moving forward: "I give her my heart but she wanted my soul" (Don't Think Twice It's All Right) and "I offer'd her my hand / She took me by the arm / I knew that very instant / She meant to do me harm" (As I Went Out One Morning). Oftentimes there's a lack of understanding: "We always did feel the same, / We just saw it from a different point of view" (Tangle Up In Blue).

However, it's probably part of destiny that you cannot hold on to love and you have to move forward and try again, because according to Dylan that's part of our condition: "You're right from your side / I'm right from mine / We're both just one too many mornings / An' a thousand miles behind" (One Too Many Mornings).

kc) The place of separation.

kca) A window.

A window usually marks the ending point of the encounter between lovers: "When your rooster crows at the break of dawn / look out your window and I'll be gone; / you're the reason I'm travelling on (Don't Think Twice It's all right), "The wind knocks my window, the room it is wet / The words to say I'm sorry, I haven't found yet" (Ballad in Plain D), "Go 'way from my window / Leave at your own chosen speed / I'm not the one you want, babe / I'm not the one you need (It ain't me, babe), "My love she's like some raven / At my window with a broken wing" (Love Minus Zero, No Limit). Dylan goes back to the window once in a while; he knows what a window means: "Standing on your window, honey, / Yes, I've been

89

here before" (Temporary Like Aquilles), "Down over the window / Come the dazzling sunlit rays / Through the back alleys, through the blinds, / Another one of them endless days" (Floater, Too Much To Ask), "Once I had a sweetheart, / Starin' out the window to the stars high above, / Time passes slowly when you're searchin' for love" (Time Passes Slowly), "Sign on the window says "Lonely," (Sign On The Window), and "He woke up, the room was bare / He didn't see her anywhere. / He told himself he didn't care, / pushed the window open wide" (Simple Twist Of Fate).

kcb) A door.

The place of separation could be also a door: "From the crossroads of my doorstep, / My eyes start to fade. / And I turn my head back to the room / Where my love and I have laid" (One Too Many Mornings); "The lover who just walked out your door / Has taken all his blankets from the floor" (It's All Over Now, Baby Blue); "She threw me outside, / I stood in the dirt where ev'ryone walked. / And after finding I'd / Forgotten my shirt, / I went back and knocked." One of Us Must Know (Sooner Or Later); Sign on the door said "No Company Allowed," (Sign On The Window); "Storm clouds are raging all around my door, / I think to myself I might not take it any more" (The Man In Me), and "You left me standing in the doorway cryin' / I got nothin' to go back to now / The light in this place is so bad / Makin' me sick in the head" (Standin' On The Doorway).

l) The distance between lovers is often expressed by the ocean.

90

The protagonist of the story accepts that it's over: "Well, the ocean took my baby / My baby stole my heart from me" (Down The Highway), "I've been out in front of a dozen dead oceans" (A Hard Rain's A-Gonna Fall), "Oh, I'm sailin' away my own true love / I'm sailin' away in the morning, / Is there something I can send you from across the sea / From the place that I'll be landing?" (Boots Of Spanish Leather), and "Now Jackie's gone sailing with trouble on his mind/ To leave his native country and his darling girl behind / Oh, his darling girl behind" (Jack - A -Roe). Plus, sometimes the protagonist of the story is conscious of the fact that there's a destiny about separation from the lover: "An' I am bound away for the sea" (Mary Ann).

Sometimes, the protagonist of the story tries to shorten distances: "I try to reach you honey / But you're driftin' too far from shore" (Driftin' Too Far from Shore); but he soon realizes that there's no point in trying: "Why am I walking, where am I running / What am I saying, what am I knowing / In this ocean of hours I'm all the time drinkin'" (Last Thoughts on Woody Guthrie). However, the ocean is not infinite: "Time is an ocean but it ends at the shore" (Oh, Sister).

In this context of separation between lovers, the music that the ocean plays is a weary tune: "The ocean wild like an organ played" (Lay Down Your Weary Tune).

m) The outlaw tastes failure in love the very next morning.

Dylan writes "Early in the mornin' / I'm callin' you to / Please come home" (Obviously 5 Believers), which extends the line "I woke in the mornin', wand'rin' / Wasted and worn out / Wishin' my long-lost lover / Will walk to me, talk to me / Tell me what it's all about" (Black Crow Blues). Those lines are all connected to "Well, I wake up in the morning / There's frogs inside my socks" (On The Road Again), "Feel bad this morning, ain't got no home" (World Gone Wrong), and "Woke up this mornin', I must have bet my money wrong (Rollin' and Tumblin').

Once again, the outlaw fails in holding on to love, which is expressed by lines like "Thinking of you when the sun comes up / Where teardrops fall" (Where Teardrops Fall), which extends the line "Early one mornin' the sun was shinin' / I was layin' in bed / Wond'rin' if she'd changed at all / If her hair was still red" (Tangled Up In Blue).

Then, the outlaw has to move on: "The sun was comin' up/ And I was runnin' down the road" (Motorpsycho Nightmare) is probably connected to "I rode straight away / for the wild unknown country where I could not go wrong" (Isis).

n) The outlaw is on his own.

At the beginning of his contemporary love-song book Dylan told us what the protagonist of this story was going to do: "I'm here a thousand miles from my home / walking a road other men have gone down" (Song To Woody), and that idea comes up once and again in Dylan's poetry, for instance, "They ask me how I feel / They'd like to drive me from this town / They don't want me around / And I walk out on my own / A thousand miles from home" (Slow Train Coming). Little by little, loving-failed experience after another, the outlaw is on his own and he starts losing himself, disappearing, which is probably why Dylan writes lines like "I'm ready to go anywhere, I'm ready for to fade / Into my own parade (Mr. Tambourine Man) and "You lose yourself, you reappear / You suddenly find you got nothing to fear / Alone you stand with nobody near" (It's All Right Ma, I'm only Bleeding). Those lines are linked to "But now mornin's clear / It's like I ain't here / She just acts like we never have met" (I Don't Believe You She Acts Like We Never Have Met), which is connected to "When you got nothing, you got nothing to lose / You're invisible now, you got no secrets to conceal" (Like A Rolling Stone), to "How does it feel / To be on your own / With no direction home / like a complete unknown" (Like A Rolling Stone), to "How does it feel / To be without a home / Like a complete unknown" (Like A Rolling Stone), and to "Walkin' through the leaves, falling from the trees / Feelin' like a stranger nobody sees" (Mississippi), just to point out some of the lines in which Dylan talks about the fact that the protagonist of the story fades, disappears, etc. Sometimes, the protagonist of the story is a shadow that can disappear easily: "But I'm looking at my shadow, I been watching the clouds up above / looking at my shadow, watching the clouds up above /Rolling through the rain and hail / Looking for the sunny side of love" (Dirt Road Blues).

The outlaw undergoes lot of difficulties to reach and to hold on to love, he goes blind or everything turns black before his eyes, sometimes he bleeds, then he's alone back on the road trying again. The outlaw is alone. Loneliness is his main feature: "I loved you then and ever shall / But there's no one here that's left to tell / The world has gone black before my eyes" (Nettie Moore).

o) The outlaw is on his own singing his song.

It is his song what helps the outlaw to keep on moving on, walking down the road: "Lay down your weary tune, lay down / Lay down the song you strum / And rest yourself 'neath the strength of strings / No voice can hope to hum" (Lay Down Your Weary Tune). That line is connected to "But my heart is not weary, it's light and it's free" (Mississippi). Let us put it this way, he's walking down that road of difficulties expressed by waters, etc., but he will survive as long as he keeps on singing his song: "Then I'll stand on the ocean until I start sinkin' / But I'll know my song well before I start singin' / And it's a hard, it's a hard, it's a hard, it's a hard / It's a hard rain's a-gonna fall" (A Hard Rain's A-Gonna Fall).

From the beginning, the outlaw's song is a love-song, that's why Dylan writes "Bird on the horizon, sittin' on a fence, He's singin' his song for me at his own expense / And I'm just like that bird, oh, oh,/ Singin' just for you, mm-mm / I hope that you can hear, / Hear me singin' through these tears" (You're A Big Girl Now), which extends the line "I got a bird that whistles / I got a bird that sings / But I ain' a-got Corrina / Life don't mean a thing (Corrina, Corrina).

Most of the time the outlaw plays his song on his own: "And if we never meet again, baby, remember me, / How my lone guitar played sweet for you that old-time melody (Up To Me) and "One of these days and it won't be long / Going down in the valley and sing my song / I will sing it loud and sing it strong / Let the echo decide if

I was right or wrong" (Silvio), which extends the line "One more cup of coffee 'fore I go / To the valley below" (One More Cup Of Coffee, Valley Below), which extends the line "I walked down to the valley" (Paths Of Victory), which extends the line "Where the home in the valley meets the damp dirty prison" (A Hard Rain's A Gonna Fall), that is —once and again— a sign of the impossibility of holding on to love: he will suffer a lot trying to reach it, and he will not be able to hold on to it, that's probably why the valley leads to a home which is a damp dirty prison.

The outlaw plays a song for the lover: "I glanced at my guitar / And played it pretendin' / That of all the eyes out there / I could see none / As her thoughts pounded hard / Like the pierce of an arrow" (Eternal Circle) is connected to "Oh, time is short and the days are sweet and passion rules the arrow that flies / A million faces at my feet but all I see are dark eyes" (Dark Eyes). Sometimes, the encounter with the lover is a song, and it doesn't last for too long: "I sang the song slowly / As she stood in the shadows" (Eternal Circle) and "As the tune finally folded / I laid down the guitar / Then looked for the girl / Who'd stayed for so long / But her shadow was missin' / For all of my searchin' / So I picked up my guitar / And began the next song" (Eternal Circle). Love doesn't last too much and then vanishes, the outlaw cannot hold on to it, that's probably why Dylan writes: "There's a song that will linger forever in our ears, / Oh, hard times, come again no more / 'Tis the song, the sigh of the weary. / Hard times, hard times, come again no more" (Hard Times), which is connected to "Tomorrow night, will it be just another memory / Or just another song, that's in my heart to linger on?" (Tomorrow Night).

Once in a blue moon, he plays the tune with the lover: "The tune that is yours and mine to play upon this earth / We'll play it out the best we know, whatever it is worth" (Wedding Song), and, eventually, someone else plays a song for him: "Hey! Mr. Tambourine Man, play a song for me / In the jingle jangle morning I'll come followin' you" (Mr. Tambourine Man).

It turns out that the song the outlaw is singing is everybody else's song. The outlaw wants other people to take his advice on how to walk down the road, that's probably why Dylan writes and sings: "May your hands always be busy / May your feet always be swift" (Forever Young), which refers to being busy and fast on the road's business, because that line extends the following: "And since my feet are now fast / And point away from the past / I'll bid farewell and be down the line" (Restless Farewell). The outlaw wants us to be careful at the stony passes of the road, which is probably why he writes and sings: "May you have a strong foundation / When the winds of changes shift" (Forever Young), which is connected to "The storms are raging on the rollin' sea / And on the highway of regret / The winds of change are blowing wild and free / You ain't seen nothing like me yet" (Make You Feel My Love).

The best thing the outlaw can wish to someone else is to play very well that tune and to sing very well that song, the song of life, because that's what life is all about in Dylan's poetry: "May your heart always be joyful / And may your song always be sung / May you stay forever young" (Forever Young).

4. Epilogue

Is Dylan the outlaw? Yes and no. No, because the outlaw is a literary character Dylan has created. Around the outlaw Dylan has built up a great metaphor of life in which each one of us is the outlaw, because each one of us is at work on the same search of love, which is probably why many people connects with Dylan's lyrics. Sounes was right when he wrote that Dylan has helped his public to explore the mysteries of life with poetic words that may indeed never be forgotten (Sounes, 2011:476). Indeed, Dylan said once: "It ain't the melodies that're important, man, it's the words." If each of us is the outlaw, then, yes: Dylan is also the outlaw, because he is one of us going down the road. He has shared with us part of his experience, but our own may very well be different.

In this context, Dylan is always talking about the same great love-story but he focusses in different aspects of it in every different love-song. Not every love-song ever written by Dylan refers to the whole great love-story we have described in the second part of this research, but probably all of them focus in one of the aspects of that great love-story which in Dylan's mind.

The reader of Dylan's poetry needs to read once all the lyrics and to establish connexions. Then, he will understand the context of Dylan's poetry. Once the reader understands the great love-story Dylan is writing about on a significant part of his contemporary love-song book, then he can re-read throughout Dylan's poetry. That's a good way to unlock some of the darkest verses of Dylan's poetry.

5. Bibliography

—Adams, Hazard. *The Offence of Poetry.* (University Of Washington Press, 2007, Washington.)

—Bob Dylan. *Chronicles: Volume One.* (Simon & Shuster, 2004, U. S.)

—Bob Dylan. *Q&A with Bill Flanagan.* March 22, 2017. Exclusive to bobdylan.com

—Bob Dylan. *Speech on MusiCares Person of the Year, 2015.*

—Mc Gregor, Craig. *Bob Dylan: A Retrospective.* (William Morrow & Company, Inc., 1972, New York.)

—Shelton, Robert. *No Direcction Home: The Life And Music Of Bob Dylan.* (BackBeat Books, 2011, U. S.)

—Sounes, Howard. *Down The Highway: The Life Of Bob Dylan.* (Grove Press, 2011, US.)

—Williams, Paul. *Bob Dylan: Performing Artist, 1960-1973, The Early Years.* (Omnibus Press, 2004, New York.)

—Williams, Paul. *Bob Dylan: Performing Artist, 1974-1986, The Middle Years.* (Omnibus Press, 2004, New York.)

—Williams, Paul. *Bob Dylan: Performing Artist, 1986-1990 & Beyond, Mind Out Of Time.* (Omnibus Press, 2004, New York.)

Printed in Poland
by Amazon Fulfillment
Poland Sp. z o.o., Wrocław